Redesign Your 9-To-5

Redesign Your 9-to-5

Advice and Strategies from 50 of the
World's Most Ambitious Business
Owners and Entrepreneurs

Created and Compiled by
BRIDGETT McGOWEN

Published by BMcTALKS Press, a division of BMcTALKS, LLC, Chandler, Arizona.

The publisher greatly acknowledges all professionals who contributed to this book.

Volume pricing is available to bulk orders placed by corporations, associations, and others. For details, please contact BMcTALKS Press at info@bmtpress.com

Cover and interior icon made by Freepick from www.flaticon.com

FIRST EDITION

Library of Congress Control Number: 202090960

ISBN: 978-0-9998901-6-5 (paperback)
ISBN: 978-1-7351192-1-2 (eBook)

Printed in the United States of America.

Dedication

To Aaron and Parker,

Thank you for going on long bike rides, playing sports in the back-yard, watching movies, engaging in spirited rounds of foosball or chess or Jenga or Life, completing all kinds of worksheets and online math modules, doing the laundry, walking to the park, running errands for me, going swimming, riding scooters, reading books, picking up restaurant take-out orders (or waiting for the doorbell to ring to signal an order had arrived), mailing packages, working out, making car wash runs—anything you could think of to give me space to complete this book (and countless other projects).

All I do is for the two of you.

Much love to you today, tomorrow, and forever.

Want to Get Published?

"You should write a book."

Either you've heard it or you've said it, but at BMcTALKS Press, we believe you should do it.

We take your dream from a great idea to a beautifully formatted book.

BMcTALKS Press is an independent publishing company that's fully committed to getting your non-fiction work published in a timely manner and providing you with a finished product that is professionally done and one of which you will be proud.

When you submit your manuscript to BMcTALKS Press, you receive personal attention, a fair price, and one of the higher author royalties in the industry.

This will be one of the most exciting experiences ever.

You have an important message. Now it's time you let everyone read it.

Visit www.bmtpress.com to schedule a complimentary ideation call and to get you FREE author's guide.

Let's print your passion!

What's the Difference?

An entrepreneur is "a person who organizes and operates a business or businesses, taking on greater than normal financial risks to do so." A business owner is "an individual or entity who owns a business entity in an attempt to profit from the successful operation of the company."

Furthermore, a business's legal status tends to be one of the key defining factors that separates entrepreneurs from other business owners; business owners tend to operate incorporated businesses.

Entrepreneurs are more likely to engage in a business venture because it presents a certain appeal, and they are more willing to take significant risks, especially those of the financial nature. However, business owners tend to have a greater focus on a business's profitability.

Dear Go-Getter,

Thank you for adding a copy of this book to your personal library. That means a lot to all the book's contributors.

We are extremely excited for you and what this step means for your personal growth and your professional future.

Congratulations on investing in yourself and valuing your development. You are SO worth it!

Now, get ready to redesign your 9-to5!

Share the Knowledge

Get this book for a go-getter FRIEND, COLLEAGUE, FAMILY MEMBER, or COLLEGE GRADUATE.

If you know of anyone who loves his/her profession and is truly talented, then it's time that person does more with that love and that talent.

Do not keep yourself a secret any longer.

Whether it's an accountant, a coach, an entrepreneur, an educator, an engineer, a marketer, a sales expert, or a medical professional ... anyone in any industry who has a passionate for doing more, in going beyond the traditional 9-to-5, or completely redesigning those work hours altogether, then this book will give that boost necessary to take the next step.

And even if business ownership is not on the radar, this one is a must-read. The stories of resiliency, pressing through when it feels like you cannot take another step, and embracing your unique power will move anyone.

Order your copies at **www.bmtpress.com/press-room**

Table of Contents

A Letter to the Reader

In the rural southeast Texas town where I grew up, you graduated high school, and if you were one of the select go-getters, then you attended college, graduated with a bachelor's degree, and some even went on to earn master's and/or terminal degrees. Others opted to stay in town or to move to Houston and experience big city life, but regardless of the route taken after high school, everyone was expected to work a respectable 9-to-5.

When I was a teen, I remember a local, who had returned to his hometown after achieving great military success, optimistically suggested to me that a career in fast food restaurant management could be my future. He was quite serious and thought that, by planting that seed in my mind, he was giving me hope for a promising path forward and that I was impressed with the notion of attaining that professional distinction. Perhaps his intent was well-meaning.

Perhaps. I am not sure.

However, that of which I *am* sure is in that moment, I felt patronized. In that moment, it felt like my academic achievements, extracurricular involvement, and overall intellect and drive painted a picture for him that was vastly different from that of which I dreamed for myself. Frankly, in that moment, I felt insulted.

I silently thought "Why is military success, like it was for you, not in my future? Why can't I, like you, serve on boards? Why can't I, like you, go on to be regarded as a successful professional speaker? Why can't I have a chance at bigger dreams?"

To suggest my professional aspirations should not go too far beyond my first job of working in fast food and implying there was little more I was capable of doing angered me. It truly angered me.

At the age of seventeen, I had not fully defined what I wanted to be as an adult. However, when he said that, I could not help but to wonder if that was the best for which I could hope. Was that the vision of success others had for me? Did my academic achievements mean nothing? Should I not bother with seeking out other opportunities?

And have *you* ever felt your talents were minimized by others?

Do you think your abilities are overlooked?

Are there days when you know ... YOU KNOW ... you can do more—that you SHOULD do more?

Every woman has a genius. Every man has a genius. Every child has a genius. Quickly find yours and act on it.

For me to truly find mine and act on it, it took me getting laid-off.

In 2013, the wife of one of my colleagues saw me present at a conference in New Orleans, and she immediately told me I needed to start my own business. I thought to myself, "Yeh, right!" The truth of the matter was I was perfectly happy with my 9-to-5 and had no intentions whatsoever of or any interest in starting a business.

However, although I was having a fantastic run with an edtech company, traveling the country and making presentations, the company went through many changes, and the next thing you know, my entire team of colleagues was disbanded; we were all laid off. In short, I knew what I loved to do, and that was to design and deliver high-energy presentations. As a result, I created my own company in April 2016.

There was a steep learning curve, though. Yes, I knew how to design presentations, own the room, and wow a crowd, but running a business was a whole other situation.

Within weeks of getting laid-off, I purchased my first two URLs; however, I sat and looked at them for months. I didn't know where to start or what in the world to do with them! I had not performed any website design work since around 2000 or so, and of course, anything I may have remembered from then was completely obsolete.

Finally, in June and with the help of that colleague's wife, both of whom have become wonderful friends, I figured out how to build a site. In July 2016, I purchased and established my LLC so others could see and regard me as a serious business.

In August 2016, I landed my first serious speaking gig. The requestor found me on thumbtack.com, reached out, and we had a phone conversation so I could learn about what the company wanted in a speaker. Because of my limited experience—not as a speaker but as a speaker who spoke on the topic the company wanted—I offered to provide a thirty-minute demo of the presentation. About a week later, I facilitated, via Zoom, the demo for three or four team members at the company, and within five minutes of the demo, the lead person who had initially contacted me stopped me and said, "I don't need to see any more. You're hired!" His colleagues unanimously echoed his sentiment.

I continued to consistently market myself as a professional speaker, submitting proposals to speak at conferences where I knew my ideal client would be in the audience and, as often as possible, where I knew big names would be on the agenda.

In November of 2017, I decided to use my maiden name, Bridgett McGowen, as my professional name because let's face it; Bridgett McGowen-Hawkins is just too long and too complicated! (When I approached my husband, Aaron Hawkins, with the idea of using my maiden name as my professional name, he said, "Fine by me—as long as the name on the checks is correct.") In June 2018, I purchased a third URL, www.bridgettmcgowen.com, using it as my primary speaker site while using the first sites, www.bmtalks.com, the vanity URL for www.bridgettmcgowenhawkins.com, for my academy services.

I have since launched BMcTALKS Academy, an online academy that offers self-paced modules and mini-courses on presentation skills plus modules on how to launch and grow a successful professional speaking business, as well as my independent publishing company, BMcTALKS Press.

The number one obstacle I faced in the beginning process of launching my business was knowing where to start, wanting to have everything perfectly in place, and worrying about naysayers.

Someone once asked me what other services and/or products, in addition to delivering keynote addresses, workshops, conference breakout sessions and webinars, did I offer. I quickly responded that I offered online modules focused on presentation skills, and before I could continue my thought about the other offerings I had on the horizon, I experienced my most disappointing memory to date as a business owner.

She all but rolled her eyes and said, "Nobody's going to buy that!"

At that point, I had been a professional speaker for more than sixteen years and a business owner for just over three and a half of those sixteen years. It wasn't so much the words that hurt, but it was the fact the words were coming from was another business owner.

And to add insult to injury, in that moment, I was her client.

As a fellow business owner, she knows there are successes but that there are also challenges. As a fellow business-owner, she knows that while most days are incredible, every day is not a picnic. As a fellow business owner, she knows the strength one possesses by the mere virtue of one making the bold decision to become a business owner but that there is always a real need for encouragement.

Or maybe she did not.

I like to think that business owners are part of a unique society where we support each other as opposed to dismiss each other, where we give recommendations as opposed to degradations, where we offer constructive guidance as opposed to careless criticism.

Or maybe she did not see anything wrong with what she said and actually thought she was being helpful.

Or maybe she knew the true impact of her words but just did not care how her response would resonate with me.

Or maybe it is was simple as what her statement inferred; she not find value in my business. And that's fine, too.

You do not have to see my vision. You do not have to believe in my vision. But do not try to crush my vision either.

A tough reality is not everyone will be in your corner, rooting for you and your business. Not everyone will be a champion for you. Not everyone will see the goal you have set for yourself.

Actually, there will be those who hope you fail, who laugh at or mock you, and those who offer no help or support but who silently observe and endeavor to minimize or who privately marvel at your success. There will be those who show indifference for your accomplishments and those who offer less-than-heart-felt congratulatory messaging because they are in your face and feel obligated to do so. And there will be those who attempt to lay claim to contributing to your success no matter how indirect, insignificant, or non-existent the contribution.

At the same time, there will be those who hope you soar, who laugh *with* you as you reminisce about how far you have come and those who will go to the ends of the earth for you because they know want only the best for you. There will be those who are as excited for and about your accomplishments as are you—so much so and with such sincerity until one would think the accomplishment was the other person's and not yours! There will be those who are impressed by you; who know you have what it takes; and who will sit on the edges of their seats, mesmerized by how you make it all happen, awaiting your next move. And there will be those who beam with pride simply because they know you or have met you for a second or two.

See your vision; pursue it full-on; and in the process, create a network of like-minded individuals who share your values and drive, and then commit to root for them, champion them, and support their visions.

For your own business launch, perform these five activities as soon as practical:

1. **Write your business plan.** You are establishing a business, so you need a plan for how it will look and operate and how you will consistently display your business to the public. At a minimum, detail your executive summary; the products and/or services you offer; your vision and mission statements; your business structure; a SWOT (strengths, weaknesses, opportunities, and threats) analysis; market analysis; sales and marketing strategy; financial projections; and your expansion and sustainability strategy. This is a lot of work, but it is your blueprint for how you will operate your business. You will be grateful you completed this early on to provide you clarity around creating a viable and profitable business. Need help? Consult with your local Service Corps of Retired Executives (SCORE) office.

2. **Establish your business as an entity that is separate from your personal self.** Both brick-and-mortar and online businesses need to

take this step to establish yourself as someone who's serious about business. This means you need to register, at a minimum, a Doing Business As (DBA) or a Limited Liability Corporation (LLC). And while you are at it, get an employer identification number (EIN) and set-up a business bank account, too. The DBA or LLC along with the EIN and the bank account are vitally important for keeping business affairs from intermingling with your personal affairs and when filing your income taxes. For brick-and-mortar businesses, these steps are more obvious. For web-based businesses, resist the temptation to *not* complete these steps.

3. **Seek out funding.** It can take time for revenue to start rolling in. For some, it can almost seem instant. For others, it requires a bit more work and effort. Assess what you need to get your business bearings—rent space, inventory, equipment, marketing, employees' salaries, etcetera—then secure funding to support a successful business launch. You can go it alone, but you do not have to go it alone by using your personal coffers in an attempt to finance your business.

4. **Assemble your team.** While you *may* be able to do everything, it is not prudent that you do. Have a team that can take care of the various aspects of your business, freeing you from having to be omnipresent. Starting out, you will wear many hats, but as you grow, that will change; it has to, or you will find yourself getting burnt out with trying to take care of every task. Besides, part of the benefit of owning a business is having the freedom to step away at any point without worry over whether it can still operate without you physically at the helm, and a team will position you to do just that. Additionally, ensure your team includes reliable legal representation. Simply put,

you do not need an attorney until you need one. Quickly identify a firm that will represent you and look out for your business interests. The amount you pay can be priceless and a fraction of what it would cost you and your business if you find yourself in a position where you need legal representation but do *not* have it.

5. Make sure others regularly see and know about you and your business. Have a constant online presence and physical presence in your community so prospective clients can know about your business; others can get to know you, advocate for your business, and send leads your way; and.you have a network of like-minded individuals from whom you can learn and grow. Some recommendations are regularly post to social media; invest in a well-designed website, search engine optimization (SEO), and advertising; volunteer at events; blog and contribute to publications; appear as a guest on podcasts; attend and present at conferences in your niche market and where you know your target audience and/or other business owners will be in attendance; and/or join local business organizations such as a chamber of commerce, Business Network International (BNI), and/or Vistage. Depending on whether you are an online business or a brick-and-mortar business, some activities will make more sense to and be more beneficial to your business than others.

Identify your passion, that which you love to do and that which comes naturally to you, and run with it. Identify your genius, and do not be afraid to speak up when you see a genius in someone else. Show others what could be. Guide them to think bigger. To be greater. To redesign their 9-to-5's ... their lives ... their futures ... because when you do what you love—and that for which others will pay you handsomely—and you never work a day in your life.

Live life with no limits. None. Recognize your power even when others do not, cannot, or refuse to see it. Push yourself to do more with your abilities even when it feels like you cannot go another step. Your dreams can be as big as you want them to be. Demonstrate to the world and for anyone who thinks you can't that you can.

You will.

You must.

B

Bridgett McGowen-Hawkins
Award-Wining International Professional Speaker, Author, and Publisher

Redesign Your 9-to-5

Remember It's a Marathon, Not a Sprint

KAREN BARNO
Intuitive Business Coach • Author • Podcaster

How I Got My Start

My dream of owning a business started at ONLY four years OLD with a child's red plastic dial-up telephone. I spent hours upon hours playing the CEO of my business. I'm not sure what I sold or did, but I was the boss lady. My red plastic phone made countless cold calls and provided the gate- way to my dream.

The Universe has many ways of showing our purpose to us— sometimes in strange ways.

Owning a business was my life-long dream, along with being a rock star.

I told anyone who would listen to me that my business would be in an office building on the top floor where it was warm. (I'm from Pittsburgh; moving to a warm climate was my goal.)

Life happens, however, and achieving our dreams doesn't always take a straight path. After a traumatic childhood filled with sexual abuse, my self-esteem was destroyed. Another challenge, a speech impediment, meant the powers in the school district decided I was "slow." That mindset locked in my career of under-performing. I graduated at the bottom five percent of my senior class, fulfilling their prediction—and my expectations.

I drank, took drugs, and did whatever it took to keep numbing the pain I was feeling.

But there was a little, tiny voice that kept playing over and over in my mind, telling me that I was here for a reason or a purpose. What purpose? No idea. The Universe had yet to reveal it.

The roller coaster of success and failure continued. During my time in the US Air Force, I discovered people who supported my dream and encouraged me to attend college.

After graduating from college, I had high-paying jobs over the years until my life collapsed again. The person within could not align with the successful person on the outside. I lost everything and was home-less.

God put an attitude of never quit in me. Quitters never win, and winners never quit. I found a man who loved and believed in me. We married and had a daughter.

The inner struggle continued. After receiving a speeding ticket that cost one hundred dollars (It's the little things that wake us up), I decided on the spot that things had to get better.

I discovered the book *Think and Grow Rich* in a used bookstore. I even had the exact amount of change in my Kmart purse to buy it. (Love the way the Universe works.) From there, I went on a twenty-plus-year journey of reading and self-introspection to heal and grow.

I founded and became the CEO of an assisted living association. My dream of business ownership was coming true. As a bonus, the association was in a warm climate.

Women began to seek advice from ME on how to start their businesses and follow their dreams. At first, I hesitated. Who am I to answer that and help with that? After early successes, I knew this is what I needed and wanted to do.

I was guiding women who were preparing to retire, looking for what to do next. They developed a multitude of strengths but weren't sure whether those strengths were their passions or tools they developed over the years to survive in the workplace.

I followed the path laid out for me while fighting my inner demons.

Then it happened again. I was stopped dead in my tracks. Negative people began to appear in my life, and I had never learned how to conquer my mindset. The hamster wheel of failure began. I was always changing my focus on who my customer was and what I was going to offer to sell. I did everything I could to sabotage my success while keeping me in pain. Sound familiar?

Next, I did what many people do. I started buying programs, coaching, anything, and everything I could with the hope that someone had the answer for me—the answer to "Who am I to own a business?" The voices from my abusive past joined the party, reminding me I was damaged goods.

I keep moving forward as there is no quit in me. I knew it's not how you start; it's where you end that matters. I still don't know that four-letter word—QUIT!

Standing at the edge of the ocean at Laguna Beach, I heard a voice say, "a teacher teaches what they have learned. Share." Turning around and seeing no one, I looked to the sky, smiled at God, and whispered, "I'm ready."

Today, I work with middle-aged women who have wandered through their wilderness called life and are ready to live in their purpose. I help them find their niche, teaching them ways to overcome their hidden fears, find their passion, and walk into their greatness.

Never forget I believe in YOU!

My Advice to Aspiring Business Owners and Entrepreneurs
There's no better time in history than now to start a business. The world has become more interconnected through technology, and that allows business owners to reach a global audience. Some examples of technological advances to help future business owners get their voices heard while spreading their newly formed business messages or ideas are podcasts, voice, websites, social media, blogs, and videos.

When you are a business owner, everyone wants to tell you about their entrepreneurial journeys. During their stories, they will say to you, in vivid detail, how they overcame certain career obstacles. All the while, each one will have an excuse or a reason as to why things didn't work out.

As you listen to their personal stories, you begin to notice a common theme between you and them. What common theme would that be you ask? Mindset!! Simple as that.

That inner voice that says "YOU can't do it, that you are not smart enough, thin enough, pretty enough, bold enough, or just not good enough to be a successful businesswoman. This inner voice holds many people back from accomplishing their dreams and following their sincere desires to make a difference in the world.

Successful people have learned how to manage their inner voice. They took the time to train their inner voice to support and encourage them during decision-making times. When their mindset goes negative, they can quickly turn it around. Mindset is an essential key to a person's success or failure. Learning how to manage your mindset will help you own your world. Some other key points to guarding your mindset are to be grateful for everything, embrace each experience as a learning exercise, and stay positive. It's easy to be or get cynical, but do not get stuck there.

Remember it's a marathon, not a sprint to the finish line. Stay on top of your game!!

Secondary to mindset, while you are on your entrepreneurial journey, are other factors that'll determine success or failure. It doesn't matter if your adventure is full-time or a side hustle; business ownership can be lonely, especially when it's time to make the hard decisions.

Having a support system in place to help you get through the good and bad times is essential. Make sure to have an encourager on your support team. Everyone needs that one person who is commonly referred to as a cheerleader, who believes in them regardless of what is happening in their life. A personal cheerleader will pick you up when you are at your lowest point and raise your confidence level to possibly its highest point no matter what other people are saying to you or about you. They believe in you and your mission one hundred percent. Cheerleaders always take the time to remind you that you can defeat, overcome, and be successful in the business world that you so desire. Keep them on speed dial! The business world is competitive, and if you want to succeed, have that one person or persons who are always available to help when your mind is clouded and going in so many different directions that you need help in filtering through your thoughts. Above all, control your thinking—change your life!

About Karen

Karen has a thirty-plus-year career as an entrepreneur and is CEO of an association she founded and built into a force in the marketplace and statehouse. She grew the association from a dream into the state's largest assisted living not-for-profit.

She developed and led the initial fundraising campaign and participated in developing the legislative and regulatory framework that is modeled across the country. She kept the association viable through two recessions and many regulatory and environmental changes.

Drawing on her skills and experience in a start-up business and in developing highly motivated tribes, she has helped women discover their authentic business niche. Karen truly enjoys assisting women in evaluating their current business models, showing them how to find their niche, and then monetizing it. Her primary goal is to help them focus on developing the tools necessary to create a more compelling future.

Karen has coached many women on how to build their six-figure and seven-figures companies, and one eight-figure business.

Karen's mantra is if you're not making money in your business, then it's a hobby.

Karen was born to coach women, helping them find their true business passion—their niche.

Karen's desire to help people was born out of her painful journey. Karen had to overcome an abusive childhood, both sexually and verbally. She graduated at the bottom of her high school class, joined the Air Force, and came out into the real world only to struggle through college. She was not able to hold a job for more than three years and simply found it impossible to erase the "I can't, I'm not worthy, I'm damaged goods" beliefs from her consciousness.

It wasn't until she invested in her personal development that Karen was able to pause and truly hear what her true essence and inner voice were nudging her to do. Eventually, she came to understand and accept her true calling—mentoring other women to overcome their past, start a business, and build a remarkable future.

After a thirty-year journey, Karen's mission is to help women define their vision of success in their business and personal life, guide them beyond the fears, and lead them toward actualizing their dream of owning a business. Karen has dedicated herself to providing resources for women to shorten their learning curve on the path of self-awareness. Through private mentoring and group mentoring programs, Karen teaches women business-building techniques that help them unlock their perfect business Niche while embracing the unique talents that will ultimately change the world around them.

Karen lives in Arizona with her husband, daughter, and bulldog named Rosie. She is an avid golfer and loves to travel with her family.

Visit Karen at https://KarenBarno.com and join Karen's free Facebook group: https://www.facebook.com/groups/PossibilitiesCafe

About Karen's Company
Barno & Associates
Intuitive Business Growth and Personal Transformation
www.karenbarno.com

Surrender to the Flow

CHRISTINA BELLMAN
CEO

How I Got My Start

I always tell people that starting my business was the first truly spontaneous thing I did in my life! It was an inspired move that was long-awaited for me... I was bursting at the seams after years of tinkering with this idea with limited resources and not feeling fulfilled by my day job. The passion fueling this energy was a very deep desire to express my creativity and make the biggest impact I could make in the short time I have on the planet! LEVO's mission—empowering users to control the ingredients in what they consume in the most imaginative ways possible—coincides with global trends that better the lives of many, and it keeps me aggressively innovating.

My Advice to Aspiring Business Owners and Entrepreneurs

Surrender to the flow, and slow down! I find that I have sometimes front-loaded my mistakes. When I first had the light bulb moment, for example, I rushed to shout it from the rooftops and proceeded to burn through some contacts that would have been much better utilized once I had more thoughtful plans together. I also (subconsciously) pushed people around me to take an interest and work on it. If it's not feeling organic or making your guts churn on any level, then I have learned the hard way to slow down and take a step back before pressing on.

About Christina

Chrissy graduated from New York University with degrees in finance, international business, and philosophy. She led the credit analysis for a pharmaceutical spin-off deal with a leading investment bank, even as an analyst, before embarking on a successful career with a Fortune 500 company where she led pricing and commercialization strategy for a new venture within the organization. Her efforts saved the program significant cost and helped capture the very first customers. Chrissy's self-funded efforts converted to a granted, non-provisional utility patent by 2017. She became a member of Entrepreneur's Organization in 2018.

About Christina's Company
LEVO
Consumer Packaged Goods
www.levooil.com

Don't Fear Change ... Embrace It!

MICHELLE BLANCHARD

Entrepreneur • OCM Leader • Executive Consultant

How I Got My Start

During the first year in graduate school, not only was I changing careers, but I also knew I wanted to honor my entrepreneurial spirit. People are my passion–I love working with great people and adding value to my colleagues and their clients. I'm also a free spirit and prefer autonomy, freedom, and flexibility. After careful—and sometimes arduous—thinking and trying to align my goals; I realized I wanted to combine my love of psychology and the neurosciences with my interest in business.

Consulting instantly came to mind—and through a lot of online research—I decided to pursue change management along with its close "cousin," strategy consulting. These two areas are usually that with which my clients need help alongside project management and program management. It has been both a rewarding and a challenging career path. The journey hasn't always been easy to put it mildly!

As a natural-born leader, I chose my current field because, for the most part, it celebrates my authenticity and core values. Honesty and integrity are also part of my work ethic in general and with my clients. They've come to know, when asking a question, the truth is what they'll receive from me (in a diplomatic, thoughtful manner). The field of industrial organizational psychology has many branches of the tree; my branches are strategy, change management, organizational effectiveness, organizational development, process improvement, and leadership development—to name a few.

As an entrepreneur, I'm always thinking about new ways of working, additional consulting areas of expertise, and new businesses I might want to start. To this point, some of my passions are arts, music, entertainment, movies, television, dancing, writing, research, screenplays, poetry, art galleries, museums, sketching, photography, color theory, visual effects, socializing, events, and anything artistic/creative!

Within the next year or two, I might implement business changes. Or I might create a new business entirely! Being a consultant, does offer the creative moments within the client engagement but not in the true sense of the artistically creative domain.

As of mid-March of 2020, I started making connections in the entertainment and the artistic/creative world. Also, I have started doing more with creative writing again.

As an entrepreneur, the possibilities are endless! Stay tuned is how I will leave this at present ...

My Advice to Aspiring Business Owners and Entrepreneurs

Be certain you're willing to endure the roller coaster ride—the many ups and downs, financial and otherwise—when you decide to embark upon an entrepreneurial journey. And what's also important is the type of business you choose to start; make certain it's truly something about which you're passionate! Research your field of interest as thoroughly as possible. Write your business plan, and review it many times, then have a mentor or other trusted adviser review it.

Periodically, reach out to other business owners to network and converse about challenges. Obtain their insights and advice. It helps to compare notes, and exchange ideas with other entrepreneurs. Being an entrepreneur is exciting but can feel "lonely" at times. It's been my experience that not all friends or family members understand the entrepreneurial spirit and mindset. Join conversations or groups with other entrepreneurs.

Take good care of your well-being—all realms of it to include physical, emotional, intellectual, spiritual and financial—so you maintain equilibrium to weather possible "storms" in your entrepreneurial journey! And, don't fear change. In fact, as an entrepreneur try to embrace change!

It's okay to change "gears" or "lanes" while driving down the entrepreneurial road. Sometimes it's important to go slow and other times, fast...but keep driving. It's very important to have your own map, too.

This will help guide you as you're driving the vast entrepreneurial road.

About Michelle

Michelle is a skilled and seasoned executive consultant, specializing in strategy, change management, organizational behavior, organizational development, and organizational effectiveness. She also has experience as a program manager and project management. People are her passion!

Additionally, Michelle used to be an executive coach but rarely takes on new coaching clients. She does engage coaching while on consulting assignments (either one-on-one or in small groups) to assist with the client/company people and their change efforts.

With any change initiative, Michelle helps with developing and implementing the strategy and the change management plan while focusing on the company/client's business goals and its stakeholders. This entails communications plans, stakeholder analysis, the project statement, change impact assessment, and project planning along with other critical deliverables and processes to name a few.

Michelle is skilled at project management and program management. She is detail oriented and keeps things organized and on-track. This can be both a blessing and a curse (she chuckles as she mentions this). Plus, with Michelle's change management background, she also views the project through the lens of the change process.

Michelle is skilled at developing people and at quickly building client relationships. As a former executive coach, and her love of people and the neuroscience, too, Michelle also specializes in talent management, leadership development, and behavioral change, and organizational behavior. She has been involved with many human capital client assignments over the course of her career.

Michelle is very creative, and with consulting, while it does offer the opportunity to create solutions for her clients, she's also creative in the artistic realms too. She's both left- and right-brained, she's also ambidextrous. Michelle is eager to possibly begin a new business within the next year or two—one which will embrace her creative interests.

About Michelle's Company
Pinnacle Consulting, also own Pinnacle Pursuits, LLC
Consulting: Pinnacle Consulting helps companies manage change. Their change initiatives impact their people, processes, and systems. Michelle, Pinnacle Consulting owner/consultant develops their strategic plans for the specific change initiative. She also works with their key stakeholders to manage the change and implement the overall plan. Additionally, Pinnacle Consulting helps with employee performance improvement, employee development, and process optimization. This also includes experience in human resources, operations, and on-boarding programs/solutions and training for new hires and consultants.

Burn the Candle at Both Ends and Light Any Other Pieces of Wick You See

JIM CERMAK
Podcast Host • Idea Guy

How I Got My Start

Helping businesses has always had a special place in my heart. If I could do it for free, I would, but my family and I like to eat; so generating income is important.

I have been planning, exhibiting at, and attending hundreds of trade shows in over twenty-five years. I have come to love and appreciate shows mostly because I see huge opportunities for both exhibitors and attendees. I think it can possibly be the best overall marketing tool because of its efficiency and versatility.

However, show after show I see companies big and small consistently make mistakes which hurt their results. And the worst part is they have no idea that they are even making these mistakes. I started thinking I can help these companies!

To confirm the size of the opportunity in front of me, I decided to do some research. I mean there's no need in putting forth all the time, money and resources to start up a business if there really isn't a true need in the marketplace.

So I attended a fairly large show (over 430 exhibitors) and decided to simply walk the show several times to see how many exhibitors drew me into a meaningful conversation. At the end, my results were two exhibitors. Yes, two. Two out of 430. Less than 0.5%. So, I thought over 99% was my market. That's bright blue ocean as far as I'm concerned!

Soon after, I started my Trade Show University podcast and Bizfire Group trade show and marketing consulting group. And immediately I saw that I was right—businesses just need better guidance. After only a handful of podcast episodes, I got a Facebook message from a regional home improvement company with a testimonial. They said after just listening to about four episodes, they made changes to how they work tradeshows and saw a 250% increase in the number of appointments booked in the same show over the previous year!

I was convinced I was on the right track. Now I am looking forward to helping small to medium-sized companies completely blow away their goals at upcoming trade shows and events and maximizing their Return on Investment.

My Advice to Aspiring Business Owners and Entrepreneurs

For those who are looking to start a business, I have two pieces of advice.

First, understand what it takes to run a successful business. This is more than just doing something you are good at and having people pay you for it! One book completely changed how I approached starting my business, and I strongly recommend this book for any entrepreneur. The book is *The E-Myth Revisited* by Michael Gerber.

This book simply and effectively shows the trap so many people fall into when starting a business. For example, most small businesses are started by someone who is good at something and often passionate about it. In the book, the author uses an example of a woman who makes wonderful pies and loves making those pies. Everyone loves her pies, and enough people, over time telling, her she should start a pie business to convince her to do just that.

Unfortunately, running a successful pie shop is far more than making delicious pies. There are finances, hiring employees, marketing, purchasing, and so much more. And all she wanted to do was make pies. She gets frustrated, burned out and, well, you can probably guess the rest of the story.

So, understand what it will take to run and grow a business! Figure out what you like and want to do, and how you can delegate the rest.

Second, if you want to start a business, then START! Do it now! Even if it's spending thirty minutes a day, do something that will help you get toward your goal. Don't put it off, and go as fast as you can. The further along you get, the more you need to do. Get up early, stay up late, burn the candle at both ends, and light any other pieces of wick you see sticking out. You will regret it if you don't.

About Jim

You know that person that loves and gets a little overly excited about what they do? That's me. People have described me as a "passionate and energetic" training and marketing professional and podcast host. I love using humor in training and helping people get "Aha!" moments that lead to better results.

Marketing was and always will be my first love with a special place in my heart for trade shows, especially helping businesses get better results through my consulting business, Bizfire Group and my Trade Show University Podcast. Listeners are reporting huge improvements in their trade show results—up to 250% year over year increases. This gets me pumped because I just want companies to win at trade shows and get excited about this marketing channel again!

My newest projects include launching a second podcast in 2020, Bizfire Business Spotlight, which is helping amazing smaller businesses get out to the world what makes them so special. I am also launching mastermind groups in the creatives and artists community, helping them turn from "starving artists" to "Thriving Artists."

Honored to be a certified PASS (Passenger Assistance, Safety & Sensitivity) Trainer and have certified over six hundred people across the country in assisting people with disabilities and proper wheelchair securement. I work to bring the best out of people and maximize training retention by helping them understand their value.

In my spare time, I love to travel with my bride of thirty years, spend time with my family, sand sculpt on warm tropical beaches, and write. I have authored and/or co-authored three books including the number one rated spiritual book of 2015 *When Will Things Start Looking Up? – A Beginner's Guide to Hope & Prayer* by Shelf Unbound Magazine in their annual review.

About Jim's Company
Bizfire Group LLC
Trade Show & Marketing Consulting, Podcast Production
www.bizfiregroup.com

A Business Owner's Three Must-Haves

BIANCA CHANDLER
Motivational Speaker • Life Coach

How I Got My Start

I have always been mesmerized by the potential people possess. As amazing as that is, what I find even more amazing is the amount of potential that goes undiscovered, unused, or undeveloped. Sometimes this is not always a choice; often it is a consequence of experiences. So, I decided to do something about it.

I began to observe the women in my life, notating patterns and behaviors. I began to pair the occurrences with the knowledge I had of each woman. Soon I realized that a lot of these patterns were found not only in the women in my immediate life but in other women as well. As I would take time to learn their stories, or even in just passing by, the themes were consistent and powerful. In our quest to be all of the things for all of the people, we often neglect self. We water everyone else while rarely saving a sufficient amount for ourselves. The more I observed this, the more I questioned why. I learned many of us are not able to grow ourselves because we are not aware that we are planted. Because we successfully produce for others, we assume we are healthy plants, but even a flower that produces for a bee has its own needs. As a life coach, I work to inspire change from the core. At our core are the seeds of all the things we produce. In order for healthy fruit to be produced, a healthy core is needed.

Each year, I host a women's retreat to combat the daily wars many women face while still having to show up for all of life's expectations. I began my business to assist other women in healing, self-discovery, goal setting, and developing the courage to take the next step. Our annual retreat strives to enhance the well-being of women by equipping them with tools that can be used in everyday life to thrive spiritually, physically, and mentally to focus on all that is ahead. Rather than feeling defeated by their circumstances, I work to help them learn that their situation is not their signature. Just because something happened to you, it should not define you.

My Advice to Aspiring Business Owners and Entrepreneurs

If you are interested in starting your own business, there are a few things I would suggest. There are plenty of places to find advice on this subject, so I will take the approach of advising the less common but essential areas—three to be exact. The first being have a great idea of who you are. Being an entrepreneur will challenge you in ways you didn't know were possible. At the end of a day, after tirelessly giving what seems to be all of you, doubt will creep in. When it does, it will move swiftly and boldly. Doubt will work a double shift to convince you that there is not enough time in the day, that your patience is not sufficient, that your product is not needed, and that your efforts are not landing on fertile ground. In times like these, your knowledge of yourself will serve as your saving grace. You will have to stand your ground in those moments by remembering who you are, whose you are, and your reason for beginning. You are needed as well as your gift.

Secondly, I would advise you to maintain a growth mindset. Regardless of how well you know yourself, also know there is always room for growth. You must be willing to be stretched rather than staying stuck. You must be willing to adapt rather than assume your way is final. You must be willing to learn from both experiences and people. Keep your ears open for lessons in the smallest of things. You must greet challenges with a mindset of strategy and conquering rather than an attack from the universe. Grow through the seasons of life rather than allowing a brisk wind to carry you away.

Lastly, I would advise having a safe zone—whether that be a specific thing you do for yourself, a specific person you call, or a specific place you go. It is imperative to have a place of refuge because rough days are inevitable, but these people, places, or things also work well for the days when you have your biggest and highest moments! Establish these things early because it will often be your peace.

About Bianca

Bianca lives with the goal of helping people improve themselves, their lives, and the world around them. Her philosophy is simple yet powerful: Living for impact: motivating, learning, improving, evolving.

She is an enthusiastic speaker and life coach who is dedicated to helping others. She works to help others discover and utilize how to best use their gifts by creating and providing professional development workshops, youth empowerment sessions, various seminars, and an annual women's retreat focused on releasing and moving "Ahead."

In addition to her work helping people improve their personal and professional lives, Bianca is invested in helping people build their spiritual lives. She is a licensed evangelist, the founder and leader of LEGO Faith as well as Rooted Youth Ministry. Both are in-depth study challenging participants to sharpen their knowledge and ability to share the gospel.

Every Monday you can find "Minute Monday," minute-long motivational content, on BiancaChandler.com and on all social media platforms. Or subscribe on her website for "Wisdom Wednesdays," weekly inspirational content that comes right to your inbox.

About Bianca's Company

bianca chandler
Women's Empowerment
www.BiancaChandler.com

Why Not Have the Best Life That You Can?

SHYLA COLLIER
Owner • Author

How I Got My Start

While I was in college at Northern Arizona University, I got an internship for marketing and public relations for credit at a community college that ended as a paid internship. Through the success of the internship, I was offered a teaching position at the community college once I completed my Bachelor of Science in Advertising and Photography at the university. Being a go-getter, during college, I started a photography business as well, which I owned for eight years. I had one of the very first business pages on Facebook. This is when my interest in social media became apparent. Facebook was a college platform when it first came about, and I just happened to be at the right place at the right time.

My internship, degree, teaching background, and experience in business ownership landed me a job in marketing with a large company that was in 17 cities. At this time, I began a women's networking group. As a 24/7 single mom, I wanted to have the flexibility to be there for my young son. This brought me to the decision to work for myself and start a marketing company. I monetized my existing networking group, opened others throughout Arizona, and merged all companies together to form Premiere Social Media.

I wanted to pursue my passion for the communications field. I have always been drawn to page layouts and putting words and pictures together. I enjoy teaching business owners about the online world and how it can transform their businesses. Empowering women in the networking groups is a great feeling. There is no cap on your income potential or expansion when working for yourself. Not only was this appealing to me but it afforded me the perfect opportunity to be a business owner as well as my own boss. I am a born leader and am happy to pass on my knowledge and experience to advance others. It is extremely rewarding to watch owners take their business to the next level. It brings me great satisfaction to help people succeed in business and in life. This was my driving force when starting Premiere Social Media. Why not work for yourself and have the best life that you can?

My Advice to Aspiring Business Owners and Entrepreneurs
It is almost impossible to give just one piece of advice when it comes to business ownership since there is so much involved. For starters, I believe a good work ethic is one of the main keys to a profitable business. Honesty is a must, and your customers will appreciate it. Be professional at all times. We will not take on a new client unless we believe that we can help the client. Provide stellar customer service and an amazing product or service. Offer them a solution rather than

just a product or service. Focus on your clients and their needs. Develop an in-depth business and financial plan to see everything outlined before you begin. An internship is a perfect place to start to gain knowledge and experience. Specialize in a certain niche; be willing to learn from your mistakes; and acquire new, helpful information. You can always move up the ladder no matter where you currently are in your business.

You are the one who makes or breaks your success. Attitude is everything. Separate yourself from your competition by owning the best business that you possibly can. Being a business owner is not easy by any means. It requires many hours of hard work and perseverance. It is very rewarding when you can sit back and look at the empire that you have created and see how many people you have helped. Reach for the stars and dream big. The sky is the limit. You can accomplish anything with hard work, persistence, and dedication. Put your mind to it. Start a business that you love and are passionate about. This is key to making your business successful.

About Shyla

Social Media Marketing expert, Shyla Collier is passionate about helping other business owners, loves photoshop, is a networking guru, and is dedicated to her clients. This Arizona native is certified in social media and completed her degree at Northern Arizona University in 2008 with a Bachelor of Science in Advertising and Photography. Her experience in business ownership, teaching, marketing, public relations, event coordination, and photography has contributed to her expertise in social media marketing. Her work ethic, creativity, and positive attitude have helped her become successful in the communications field. She has more than thirteen years' experience in marketing.

Shyla taught at a local community college for several years. Her in-depth social media trainings have been held for other groups at many chamber of commerce events and to thousands of business owners and staff.

Shyla Collier is the published author of *Social Media Key to Credibility* and is a contributing author in the Amazon best-selling book *When You're Done Expecting*, which was endorsed by the co-founder of the Make-A-Wish Foundation.

Shyla is the owner and founder of Premiere Social Media, a worldwide marketing company, located in Mesa, Arizona. Premiere specializes in social media management and training, website and graphic design, search engine optimization, and women's networking groups throughout Arizona. Premiere Business Networking forms teams of power partners to take business owners to the next level. These business groups incorporate networking, leads, and social media marketing. Premiere Social Media is your one-stop-shop for all your online marketing needs.

Our mission is to help business owners nationwide build credibility, improve their online presence, and teach women how to network and support one another to succeed.

Shyla lives with her ten-year-old son in the Phoenix, Arizona area. She loves being the best mom that she can be by creating memories with him that will last a lifetime. She has been involved in charitable organizations and has been featured in numerous magazines, newspapers, podcasts, and radio shows.

About Shyla's Company
Premiere Social Media
Marketing
www.premieresocialmedia.com

Everything Starts in the Mind

ROY COTTON, JR.
Transformation Specialist • Host of Love & Inspiration Radio Show

How I Got My Start

For as long as I can remember, I have always loved to inspire, and I have inspired family members, friends, colleagues, and millions during my lifetime. Many of my friends would find comfort and be inspired after sharing their concerns or challenges with me. My friends and associates often come to me and ask for advice because they feel comfortable and at peace after speaking with me.

I remember back in 2003, as a teen, I would go over to a friend's house on Friday afternoons and we would listen to the latest music in R&B, hip hop, dance, reggae, and more.

At that time, I was a disc jockey who loved listening to music and who also played for a few house parties.

On one occasion, I told my friend that one day I would become a radio host, be able to play my music for a wide audience and become well known. He laughed and shrug the idea off. I told him to watch and we will see what happens. As they say, the rest is history; I manifested my dream.

I started as a radio host of my own radio shows back in 1994 on my beloved Caribbean island, St. Maarten. When I moved to England in 2002, I took a break from radio broadcasting. In 2007, however, my love for broadcasting was reignited when I felt inspired by God to go back into radio broadcasting.

What prompted this desire you may ask? Whilst studying at a university in the Netherlands, my parents experienced challenges in their marriage, which, unfortunately, led to their divorce in 1997. My parents' divorce had a profound impact on my life. Imagine while you're growing up, you were always happy to know that your parents are married and are not a divorce statistic as many of your friends' parents. Then suddenly, while being a student overseas, you get the news that your parents are divorced. Imagine how shattered you'd feel. That was my reality. So this experience prompted my desire to help couples and families build stronger relationships and inspire others to live meaningful lives. This passion to transform lives contributed to me returning to the airwaves.

In my musings about the name of a new radio show which would inspire the lives of many, express love, and build stronger relation-ships, the name Love & Inspiration was dropped in my spirit. I knew that when the name Love & Inspiration dropped into my spirit, it came directly from God. I knew instinctively that the name and radio show would have a significant impact in the lives of many from that day onward.

On February 11, 2007, the Love & Inspiration Show premiered on the student radio station at University of Hertfordshire where I was a student in England, broadcasting to a student population of 23,000 students and online listeners around the world. Love & Inspiration did extremely well within its first year; this led to me being nominated in the categories of Best Male Presenter, Best Interview, and Best Entertainment through the annual Student Radio Awards supported by BBC Radio 1 and Global in the United Kingdom in July 2008.

I recognize that even though between 2011 and 2012, I experienced self-doubt regarding the show as it seemed like no one had interest in listening to it, I made the right choice to start Love & Inspiration. It was also a challenging time getting sponsors for my show. I practically felt like throwing in the towel.

However, my beautiful wife, Nicole, believed in me and my radio show. She urged me not to discontinue my show but to hold on to it as she recognized Love and Inspiration's value and that it had the capacity to transform the lives of millions while being monetized. As it is rightfully said, "It's good to listen to your wife," which I did, so I kept the radio show and persevered.

Presently Love & Inspiration is a successful thirteen-year-old radio show produced by me and is now syndicated in the New York City area on Bshani Radio. With only one month on the station in April 2019, Love and Inspiration ranked number four with 1.3 million downloads. In June 2019, Love & Inspiration had 1.6 million listeners and ranked second place; and in July 2019, it had 1.9 million listeners and ranked first place. As of May 2020, Love & Inspiration has a listenership of 2.2 million worldwide.

As I reflect on how far I have come during the past thirteen years, I can boldly say "Thank God for inspiring me in 2007 with the name Love & Inspiration and for me heeding the call. Today, I am building stronger relationships and transforming the lives of many, one heart at a time."

My Advice to Aspiring Business Owners and Entrepreneurs

It is an honor to share invaluable advice with you in terms of starting your business or manifesting your idea.

- I'd say, go to God in prayer, and ask Him what is His will for you so that you are able to bless and transform the lives of His people in this world.
- Be attentive to the still inner voice that comes from God who inspires you with that business idea you are to execute for His glory.
- Act on the business idea, write the vision down, and run with it according to Habakkuk 2:2.
- Sometimes a business idea comes into our minds, and we think about it a for short while. We get distracted or don't act on it, and before you know it, it disappears, or someone else runs with the idea. According to my good friend Bennie Randall, Jr, CEO of Bshani Radio in New York, "Everything starts in the mind; it's an idea. Everything starts with an idea. It starts internally."
- Clarity is power. In order to successfully reach your goals with your business and have a far-reaching impact in the lives of clientele, get clear on what you want to achieve with your business.

- Start your business from a place of believing in yourself and your product/services; creativity; innovation; love; happiness; kindness; peace; faithfulness; self-control; patience; honesty; integrity; thinking long-term; solving problems for people; respect for yourself, staff, and clientele; thinking big; focusing on opportunities; getting paid for results, not time; expecting to succeed; and believing that you are more than enough and can do all things through Christ who strengthens you.
- Be committed, and consistently execute your business to achieve its vision and mission statement.

About Roy

Roy Cotton, Jr. is an empathic, visionary, interpersonal and professional development coach; youth specialist; motivational speaker; radio show host; and transformation specialist who is genuinely interested in empowering others. As a global difference maker, he is fully dedicated to accomplishing his life's purpose to transform millions of lives. He is an entrêpreneur; a great communicator, and columnist of "Student Vibes, Love & Inspiration and Keeping Safe with Roy" in The Weekender of The Daily Herald on St. Maarten.

He is an entrepreneur, a great communicator, and columnist of "Student Vibes, Love & Inspiration and Keeping Safe with Roy" in "The Weekender" of *The Daily Herald* on St. Maarten.

Roy was born and raised on the beautiful island of St. Maarten and educated at the Milton Peters College. He went on to study extensively in Europe, primarily in London and The Hague.

He holds a postgraduate certificate in Inter-cultural Group Therapy and Counseling from the University of Goldsmith, London, United Kingdom; studied person-centered and psycho-dynamic counseling at the University of Hertfordshire, Hatfield, United Kingdom; is trained in systemic counselling with families and couples at the University of Birbeck, London, United Kingdom. Roy is also a graduate of the prestigious Global Excellerated Business School for Entrepreneurs, which has positioned him to be a successful entrepreneur.

He successfully works with his wife Dr. Erna Mae Francis-Cotton, as a co-therapist in pre-marital and marriage therapy sessions. He also provides health coaching as a Lifestyle Prescriptions® Medicine Health Coach to transform his clients' lives. Roy is truly a man of God with a mission in life to uplift humanity.

Roy is a former instructor and personal development coach to police, prison guards, customs, and immigration recruits within the Ministry of Justice. He has coached the young, local cricket players aged thirteen to twenty-five of West Indies Cricket Association on St. Maarten.

He is the Head of the Y2X (Youth2Xtreme) media team for their radio show, Fresh. He provides motivational and inspirational sessions to teachers and students at various high schools which yield transformational results.

He is a former instructor at the University of St. Martin where he taught freshman students in the one-credit course, Freshman Development Seminar, how to effectively cope with college and university life. He also taught students in the three-credit interpersonal communication course to enhance their interpersonal communication skills within their work, family, love, and friendship relationships.

He has a heart for young people and believes we are relationship-oriented beings. He wants to see young people succeed in what they do and feel appreciated.

Roy also provided transformational team building sessions to Immigration and the St. Maarten Correctional Services within the Ministry of Justice.

On October 31, 2019, after serving his birth land St. Maarten within the Ministry of Justice for eight years in Child Protection, the St. Maarten Justice Academy and the Miss Lalie Youth Rehabilitation Center, Roy decided to step out in faith and become a full-time entrepreneur.

He made a conscious decision to trust God and believe that He would make a way for him as God had proven His faithfulness toward him while living in Curacao for two years, Europe for 14 years; six years in Holland, and eight years in England. God continues to be faithful to him while back on St. Maarten since August 2010.

Roy conducts motivational speeches and transformational sessions alone or along with his wife to individuals, CEOs and organizations globally who are hungry for inspiration and transformation.

About Roy's Entities

Lifestyle Prescriptions® Health Centre St. Maarten, Caribbean
https://lifestyleprescriptions.info/stmaarten/
Email: transformationspecialistcotton@gmail.com

Love & Inspiration with Roy Cotton Jr.
https://www.bshaniradio.com/love--inspiration
Email: rc.loveandinspiration@gmail.com

You Have to Be The Little Engine That Could

WENDY COULTER

Brand Strategist • President/CEO of Hummingbird Creative Group, Inc. Founder of the NC Women Business Owners Hall of Fame

How I Got My Start

In the early 1990's, after I graduated from the College of Design at North Carolina State University with degrees in architecture and industrial design and a minor in communications, I entered the workforce for a bit, working for a very small non-profit. In my job, I was able to explore some projects related to product design, but I also jumped into marketing, graphic design, and public relations activities to help build the organization's support and fundraising because that was a bigger need. I learned so much in my role from creating a consistent identity for the organization, developing graphics and promotional tools, promoting our events, placing public service announcements (PSAs), and enticing the media to cover the organization in an effort to get the word out about what we were doing in the local community. It was very rewarding for a while, and

I loved the small team I was working with each day. However, as time went on, I learned my most important HR lessons that would follow me throughout my life—to respect everyone around me, to show gratitude for my team, and to ensure my employees always get paid for their work. I recall sitting in staff meetings where my boss announced our performance for the week on a scale from A to F, as if we were in grade school, which destroyed everyone's morale and certainly created unnecessary conflict and competition. I was subjected more than once to degrading comments from him, which I felt were best to ignore in order to stay employed. In less than a year in that role, when it became a regular practice to call the bank to make sure sufficient funds were available to cover my paycheck, I was the first team member to make the decision to move on. Within two weeks, the entire team had left the organization. With no job, in the early fall of 1995, I walked into the Cary Chamber of Commerce Expo and signed on my first three clients. Acknowledging my ability to sell, which I learned through working in my family's business as a child, I was excited to found my new company, Hummingbird. With a desire to escape the workforce and show respect to everyone I work with and for, I was able to put my own ideas to work, creatively solving problems for small businesses through graphic design, marketing, and PR services.

My Advice to Aspiring Business Owners and Entrepreneurs
"I think I can... I think I can... I think I can..."
 ~The Little Engine That Could

All my life, people have called me determined. I walked early—my mom would tell you I never even crawled; I just ran. I never thought about being determined as a kid, it was just who I was... at age sixteen, though, I found myself sitting in a room very frustrated. I was on Duke campus for the North Carolina Writing Scholarship competition. We had two and a half hours to write an essay; the paper in front of me read "write about a work of literature that has inspired you in your life." As an honors AP English student, I had read all the classics— *Huck Finn, The Odyssey, Lord of the Flies, MacBeth, Pride & Prejudice, Beowulf, The Old Man and the Sea,* and the list goes on. A full two hours went by, and I had not put one word on the paper. I had a total writer's block...Then it hit me—in the last thirty minutes, I wrote about a book that had truly influenced my life that I could defend properly in an essay–*The Little Engine That Could.* This children's book about a little Blue Engine that "thought she could" won me a writing scholarship to college and in that half hour, I learned the most important lesson I needed to learn about business ownership!

My advice to someone considering starting a business is that you have to be ready to persevere no matter what—you have to be The Little Engine That Could!

Now, there are several engines that we meet in the classic children's story, starting with a red engine that has stalled out.

You'll Meet The Red Engines
I started Hummingbird in 1995. I was twenty-four years old, and the youngest business owner I knew at the time. By 2002, running a business without having ever been in the industry or knowing anything about business finances had put me personally deeply in debt. At this point in time, my accountant, some family members, and

many advisors were red engines... They were stalling out on me, telling me I should give up the business and file bankruptcy. I owed vendors, credit card companies, and family money.

I got married in September 2001, and in the spring of 2002, I sat down with my new husband, James, and told him how much trouble "we" were in. My search for a bankruptcy attorney began the next week. I decided to meet with three attorneys. Luckily, the third one asked me a life-changing question: "If you did not have the debt, would your business be successful today?" My answer was yes, and he discouraged me from filing bankruptcy. Shortly thereafter, I met an angel at a Cary Chamber of Commerce meeting—a CPA who helped me formulate a plan. With the income from my "successful business," I paid off my mountain of debt in under a year and a half and have proudly been debt-free ever since!

You'll Meet The Yellow Engines

In any growing business, employees come into play. Although today my team is super strong, I have to admit I've hired several shiny new yellow passenger engines. These shiny engines look so perfect on the surface, but they really are not interested in the business's success. And in the creative industry, they are all shiny—that's their job.

One of my first hires seemed so perfect like the shiny yellow engine. We worked together through a move into a new office and growth to five employees, and everything was going really well. One morning, she was late to work, and in mid-afternoon, I realized she had been gone again for hours without telling anyone where she was going. She came back after having been gone for over four hours. I called her into my office to see what had happened and talk to her about why she did not let anyone know where she was. She proceeded to stand up, pick up the chair she was sitting in, and sling it across the room at me in a rage, leading to her dismissal. Over the next couple of weeks, she would come to the office and meet my other team members outside on a daily basis. I decided to pull together my remaining staff for a team building retreat on a Friday afternoon. I arrived at a local park with the moderator, but none of my team was there on time—they were about a half-hour late. Once everyone arrived, we began the meeting, and the former employee was on the park train, riding around and around the park throughout our meeting. I determined that she was trying to confront me alone at the park, and all my team members knew it. Needless to say, I had to make a tough decision to terminate the employees who were involved in order to move forward.

Two other shiny yellow engines who worked for me quickly became best friends—they treated the business like it was their own, perhaps too much! One was the other's direct report, and when the manager approached me with some issues she was having, I let her know to cover them at the review she was having the following week. I had not learned to always have two people in reviews yet, so they had their meeting, and her direct report put in her notice. Within one week of her two-week notice, our office was burglarized and ransacked, and her space was the only part of the office not touched. When she left, she began her own agency and proceeded to call on my clients in an attempt to steal the business. However, every client she called on defended Hummingbird and immediately called me.

We did not lose a single client, and she immediately lost credibility in the local business community.

You'll Meet The Great Big Strong Black Freight Engines

We all meet a lot of great, big strong businesspeople who may or may not be able to help us in business even though they say they can… I've met a few "mentors" along the way who did not turn out to be what they seemed. Beware of the "big, strong freight engines."
For example, I met a woman several years back who took me under her wing. She had grown a business to the point of successfully selling it and seemed to have a high business acumen when I met her. She told me she could help me build my business, and it began as a wonderful relationship with her introducing me into one phenomenal new account and helping me win several awards.

On the other hand, it began as a rough relationship on a personal level. As my "mentor," she told me my hair was too long, my neck-lines were too low, and my skirts were too high. She made fun of the shoes I wore and told me to get my eyebrows waxed and my nails done more often. The very confident young woman I had always been now looked in the mirror every day wondering if I was going to see her and what she would have to say. She went so far as to tell me that another businesswoman I highly respected in the community would never take me into a meeting because of how I dressed. I have since parted ways, but from all this I learned a valuable lesson—people are always judging, and we have to be aware of that in business. Today, I confidently look in the mirror again…and I'm proud of what I see.

You'll Meet The Black Rusty Tired Old Engines

I've finally learned in business that it will really bring you down if you choose to do work for black, rusty, old engines. No matter how young you are in business, one important piece of advice to heed is to take the time to wisely choose with whom you work!

Hummingbird had a client in the local construction industry. He was a super-dynamic guy with a successful company, and his stories were so engaging until my whole team was mesmerized. However, every time we met, it was such a chore to get through the meeting with a good resolution of goals and next steps. This guy was all over the place, which is pretty par for the course when you are working with the C-suite, but this relationship was extra challenging. One day, he was sitting in the conference room with me for a meeting. He had brought his young daughter with him, and I could smell the alcohol on his breath; this took me back to my younger days growing up in a household with an alcoholic. After the meeting, he left, and I cried for her a bit, then I went on with my day. A couple weeks later, we had another meeting. This CEO sat down at my conference room table, pulled out a bottle of pills, and chased several of them with a beer he pulled out of his bag. I was shocked and asked him to leave. He looked at me stunned. I have not seen him since, but I did talk to one of his staff members after the incident, and she told me I had caused a positive turn in his life. I really hope so—for his daughter's sake!

This story is uncommon, and perhaps the more common situation is dealing with people who do not respect you for that for which they hired you or are just not a good match for your corporate culture.

The best thing you can do is figure this out during the sales cycle and make a conscious choice to "work with only those people you know, like and trust!"

Be The Little Blue Engine!
So, I've made it through these challenges because I am determined to always be the Little Blue Engine. My husband tells anyone we meet that Hummingbird is still around twenty-five years later because I just won't ever give up—no matter what.

The best way I know to stay the Little Blue Engine is to continue to be willing to change and adapt at every turn. This is very important every day but most of all in a crisis. From the dot com bubble and the attack on the World Trade Center, to the COVID-19 crisis, I've had to continuously adapt in order to overcome, but most of all, I never gave up!

The other part of this story that we should all take note of in business is that there were three trains in the story that opted to not get involved, but the little blue engine did! As a good friend of mine in business, Patty Geiger, recently reminded me, "This American fairytale has a simple message: always be humble and kind ... show compassion ... take action from a place of love." And the Little Blue Engine smiled and seemed to say as she puffed steadily down the mountain, "I thought I could... I thought I could... I thought I could!"

About Wendy

Before she could even read, Wendy Coulter was working in the family shoe store. Back then, promotions and marketing meant going on the radio to play guitar or riding an elephant in the town parade.

A lot's changed, but entrepreneurship certainly runs in the family. After graduating from the School of Design at North Carolina State University with degrees in architecture and industrial design and a minor in communications, Coulter entered the workforce for a bit. But in 1995, she founded the business with a desire to put her own ideas to work, creatively solving problems for small businesses.

For Wendy, the hummingbird symbolized what she wanted to do: fly. Hummingbirds can fly forwards, backwards, sideways, and upside down. Over two decades later, Hummingbird Creative Group is doing it, thanks to a diverse and dedicated staff. And Wendy is still intent on sitting down personally with each client to understand the essence of their brand. Her passion is to shift brand equity from the business owner to the business entity, which strengthens the company's promise, presence, and profitability over time.

With over twenty-five years of sales and marketing experience and over twenty years of design and branding experience, Wendy Coulter's passion is to help businesses more effectively communicate their positioning, differentiate their brands, and grow revenue. She has grown Hummingbird with a commitment to move marketing initiatives forward for clients in a way that profoundly and positively impacts all areas of their businesses, and she encourages her team to exchange egos for listening, connecting, and driving engagement to help clients live their brands as much as they communicate their brands.

Under Wendy's leadership, the company has won the Pinnacle Business Award from the Raleigh Chamber of Commerce as well as Business of the Year, Employer of the Year, and Successful Achievement awards from the Cary Chamber of Commerce.

Wendy's team at Hummingbird has also won numerous design awards including Davey Awards in 2014, 2015, 2016, and 2019; Marcom awards in 2014 and 2019; three Healthcare Advertising Awards in 2018; a MOMBA award in 2014; two Mature Media Awards in 2013; an RBMA Quest Award in 2010; two MAME Raleigh Awards in 2009; silver and bronze international Summit Awards in 1999, 2000, and 2008; two American Corporate Identity Awards and two American Corporate Identity awards in 2007; three American Corporate Identity awards in 2006; and Triangle ADDY Awards in 2004 and 2005.

Wendy has won numerous awards for her civic work in the local business community including a 2020 Enterprising Women of the Year Award given by Enterprising Women Magazine.

She is a 2016-2017 graduate of Leadership Cary and was named the 2015-2016 NAWBO-Greater Raleigh Woman Business Owner of the

Year, a Top 50 Entrepreneur and Woman Extraordinaire by *Business Leader Magazine*, and has received Women in Business and 40 Under 40 Leadership awards from Triangle Business Journal. The company was also honored with the NAWBO Greater Raleigh Corporate Sponsor of the Year Award in 2013-2014.

Coulter founded the NC Women Business Owners Hall of Fame in 2018 and is a 2020 inductee. She is a past-president of National Association of Women Business Owners (NAWBO) Greater Raleigh and the North Carolina Executive Roundtable.

Wendy frequently presents on topics including leadership, business growth, and branding.

About Wendy's Company
Hummingbird Creative Group, Inc.

Hummingbird Creative Group helps build business value through building brand equity through clear communication of brand differentiation. The company is an award-winning, full-service branding agency that helps companies define brand strategy; develop sustainable brand messaging; and implement marketing tactics through advertising, graphic design, sales enablement, public relations, and online marketing services.

hummingbird-creative.com

Challenge Yourself and Take Chances

NICOLE M. D'AGOSTINO
Owner • Creative Planner • Designer

How I Got My Start

I started my events planning business, Nikki's Creative Designs, LLC, back in 2007 to create additional income to provide for my children who were small at the time. I love planning and creating events and turned my passion into a small event planning business. My business had a slow start taking off; I had one to two events every six months. Then when the economy took a dive in 2009, I stopped operating my business and decided to focus on my full-time corporate job in higher education. From time to time, family or friends would ask me to create or design invitations, banners, and centerpieces for their milestone celebrations.

In 2015, I started planning my vow renewal ceremony, and my creativity and passion for planning kicked into overdrive! I knew that

I had to take the necessary steps to re-launch my business. I was hearing stories of individuals, couples, and corporations looking for an event planner who had an air for creating events that were memorable and who incorporated their visions rather than the events just being all about what the planner says.

I re-launched my business in 2016, did a name change, and was now operating under the name Events by Nicole Monea, LLC. I felt excited, driven, and nervous as I didn't know if my business would be successful this time around. Was I taking all the right steps to ensure success? And could I give it my all? Those were the questions that stuck out to me.

I incorporated marketing, networking, and a website, which I did not do the first time around. I held an event planning open house and launched all social media pages to get me out in the event planners world. I also enrolled in a small business entrepreneurship certificate Program through Fresh Start Women's Center to learn the basic fundamentals of owning and operating a business the right way and how to make your business successful and sustainable.

The success thus far has been not far from amazing! I have a client base of new and returning customers who hire me for their milestone events that range from weddings, anniversaries, birthdays, baby showers, and graduations to dinner parties.

My Advice to Aspiring Business Owners and Entrepreneurs

One piece of advice I would give anyone looking to start a business would be to educate yourself, take the necessary courses, attend workshops, and invest in the time to make sure that you do everything correctly. Challenge yourself, and take chances. Pray for your business daily! Have a strong support group. Realize that sometimes you have to be your own cheering team; others may not get it and that is OKAY. Set realistic goals, and don't be hard on yourself if you don't hit them.

About Nicole

I am a successful small business event planner who started her small business in her home in 2007 and re-launched it in 2016. My background is finance and education. My passion is creating events for my clients that leave a lifetime of memories. I have four beautiful children, Aliyah, Akil, Rovelle and Nicholas, for whom I started my business to leave a legacy and something that they could inherit and run in the future. I have an amazing and supportive husband, Nick, who pushes me daily to give 100 percent in my business. My parents, Ron and Rosemary Abram, are also my support system along with my dearest and closest friends and business colleagues. I have been tremendously blessed to work in corporate America as a higher education advisor while focusing on my dream. My future goal is to one day be featured in *Forbes Women's Magazine* as one of the top African American event planners.

About Nicole's Company

Events by Nicole Monea
Event Planning
www.eventsbynicolemonea.com

Take a Chance on Yourself ... Choose YOU!

ELIZABETH DILLON
Keynote Speaker • Revolutionary Change Agent • Navy Wife

How I Got My Start

Over the last few years, I have acquired some pretty amazing national public speaking mentors. They all agree that, as a speaker, you need to relate to your audience and vice versa. No one really wants to hear all of your work accomplishments. The audience wants to hear your struggles and how you triumphed over adversity. Alex Dorr from Reality-Based Leadership said that their data are backing this theory of connecting via sharing your experiences. In *Own the Microphone*, I shared about a traumatic car accident that changed my life. In this book, I want to give you a view into the life of Team Dillon today.

I am married to Petty Officer First Class Myles Dillon. Last year we were balancing six jobs on top of processing more grief than we could handle. And 2020 doesn't seem to be getting any easier as we are now experiencing a global pandemic and an economic recession. The Navy informed Myles that he is tagged for active duty. Another new chapter and life changing experience, but we will work hard and do our best—no matter what comes our way.

As I was developing my intro for my speech in February, I wanted to get REAL and share this intense journey and how far I've come.   So, let's dive in and see what I shared with Michiana Human Resources Association (MHRA) in February. I'm going to back it up to August of 2018. In eight short weeks, all of our grandmothers had died, and our families were in complete chaos. Unfortunately, for me, I had to stuff my grief deep down because I had a keynote presentation for the Michiana SHRM Leadership Summit for which to prepare. I cried between practice sessions, and when the day came, I got up there and put on a brave face to get the job done. As we started to move forward with our lives and process the grief, we found out in January of 2019 that we were pregnant. We were so happy to bring some light to our families after being in deep, consuming grief.

I want to share some light and love, so I'm going to tell you about our first ultrasound together. This story still makes me giggle. My husband came with me to an ultrasound, and there we learned that there were two yolks in the sac. Yes, you read that right! We were going to have identical twins. My husband about fell out of his chair—he was so shocked. He even shouted at the ultrasound tech asking, "Are there two babies in there?" She replied with "That's what it looks like ..."

I was eight weeks pregnant when Myles checked into Navy Drill Weekend and I checked in to the ER. I was informed that I was most likely having a miscarriage. I called Myles, and he informed his command. They understood his concern and allowed him to come home to be with me and make up his drill at a later date. It was a life-changing experience for the both of us, but I'm glad that I had him as my partner. As we again started moving forward and processing our grief, I was scheduled for a surgery in March of 2019. I kept thinking to myself "Does everyone else have years like this?" As intense as it was, we never gave up. We balanced six jobs while dealing with more than most people could imagine.

Meanwhile, there was so much more going on in the background that people didn't know about. On top of all of the other life events that had taken place, I had been dealing with bullies. I had been informed that I didn't have the right to call myself a keynote speaker on LinkedIn because I wasn't a paid national traveling speaker. There were times when I was no longer sure that I should pursue this path, and I started to feel broken beyond repair. I knew that I loved speaking, sharing my stories and advocating for others. I knew if I didn't chase my dream, I would settle in life. I knew it was time to heal, learn, grow, and flourish in this new capacity. I was so grateful when HR professionals excitedly gave follow-up feedback after my presentations. They wanted me to know that they were implementing new changes in their organizations. One professional said that she not only came up with a great competitive advantage, but she was able to get her business case approved by the C-suite to implement Friday summer hours, giving more flexibility and time back to their employees. It went to so well that they will continue this practice in the coming years YAY! What I have learned from all of this is simple.

I AM a woman! I AM a millennial! I AM an entrepreneur!

I AM a keynote speaker, and I was BORN to INSPIRE others by sharing my knowledge, experience, and others' stories. I CAN make it through anything, and I will overcome any obstacles that get in my way. I am so much stronger and greater than others give me credit for.

My Advice to Aspiring Business Owners and Entrepreneurs

First, surround yourself with cheerleaders who will root for you along the way. My favorite cheerleader is my next-door neighbor, Connie. She is this sassy, petite, wonderful, retired woman who has become my adopted grandmother. She can see my passion when I speak, and she lights up when I tell her of my achievements. She has supported me through the tough times, and I couldn't imagine a better cheerleader on my side. We cried together when I showed her my first book. We said she would be the grandma to accept the book on behalf of all of the ones who were no longer here.

Second, there will always be people who doubt your ability to reach your goals and chase your dreams. I've said for years I was inspired by Angelina Jolie in *Beyond Borders*. I would love to be a United Nations Goodwill Ambassador. As I've found my love for public speaking, I thought it would be a goal to one day be on the *The Talk* or *The View*. I would love to bring an HR perspective to the group and a voice for the people. Those dreams and goals may or may not happen, but I won't let anyone tell me that I can't. Only I can determine my fate. As hard as it may be, you have to keep fighting for you and your dreams. Jim Rohn said, "If you are not willing to risk the usual, you will have to settle for the ordinary." Who wants to be ordinary and settle for it? I don't want to live my life with regrets, and I wish the same for you. Take a chance. Invest in yourself. Chase your dreams. Choose YOU!

About Elizabeth

With her public speaking passion growing, she created a consulting company called Revolutionary HR where she is CEO, lead consultant, and public speaker. In her free time, she has done pro bono résumé, interview, and LinkedIn consulting for veterans and the unemployed.

She is currently the Michiana SHRM vice president of membership and is working her way up to president in the future. Starting in 2020, Beth will be working for the HR Indiana State Council. The organization has created a position that will allow her to work with the Membership and Workforce Readiness Committees. Beth will be traveling throughout the state to educate others on the HR Indiana and SHRM Foundation's initiative to reintegrate veterans back into the civilian workforce.

About Elizabeth's Company

Revolutionary HR LLC

Business Consulting

http://www.revolutionary-hrllc.com/

Ask Questions, Then Ask Some More

SITHARI EDIRISOORIYA, D.C.
Chiropractic Physician

How I Got My Start

I started my business after working for over a year and a half at a multidisciplinary practice. After eight months of working at the practice, my boss told me he had bought another location to expand the business. He wanted me to work at both locations. I didn't want to start finding patients for the new location and maintain my new schedule. Nevertheless, I took time to think about the new change.

At the time, I was scared of starting a practice. This was an excellent way of facing the challenges of starting a new practice without the financial burden. Later, I told him I would be happy to work at both locations. Initially, it was a struggle. He made a new website, new phone number, and different name for the second location. It took almost two months before I started getting new patients.

Soon, I had regular patients and a stable practice. Still, I felt exhausted. I was working at two locations, six days per week. Six months later, my boss told me our working relationship shouldn't continue and asked me to buy the second location. I was stunned. I was growing that practice; however, I didn't want to buy the practice. I realized I was ready to start my own. I learned how to build something from nothing.

I told my boss a few days later that I wouldn't buy him out. His next words left me speechless. He told me he had changed his mind and wanted me to stay. I didn't know what to think. We had a long conversation, and I said I would continue working, but we couldn't have this same conversation again. He agreed. I went home that day and discussed everything with my family. We agreed that this was not a healthy working environment. My family also agreed that I should leave his business.

The next day, I started putting together my business plan. I looked at logos, searched for places to practice, and applied for a business license. Three months later, my boss and I had a conversation where we both realized our working relationship wasn't productive anymore. He gave me a few options for how long I wanted to continue working there. That helped with my process of finding my new location. I was able to start my practice very quickly and have a smooth transition.

My Advice to Aspiring Business Owners and Entrepreneurs
I have advice and questions for anyone starting a new business to think about.

When choosing a name, pick something succinct and easy to remember. The name of your business should incorporate the service you provide and distinguish you from other competition. Choose a name that is scalable.

Your location should be consistent with your style of business and image. What are the demographics of your clientele? Is there a strong economic base in the community? What skills do you need, and are people with those talents available? Is there heavy foot traffic in the area? Is there any competition nearby? Are there any services you may want conveniently located? What are the zoning restrictions?

Keep your overhead low! This is crucial when you are starting out and have a large amount of expenses. You should have a business plan prepared with a timeline for expansion.

What is your current financial situation? Do you have the funds necessary to start your business? Will you need to take out a loan? Do you know how much money you will need?

If you are in the planning stages, Service Corps of Retired Executives (SCORE) can help you prepare a business plan and financial plan. They have business mentors that can meet with you and help you through the process. SCORE is a free volunteer-based business mentoring partner of the U.S. Small Business Association (S.B.A.) and has chapters across the country.

Contact your local chamber of commerce. It is a great resource for networking and building relationships in the community as well as advertising and building your brand.

About Sithari

Dr. Sithari Edirisooriya earned her Bachelor of Science with honors from Youngstown State University (YSU) in Ohio and her Doctor of Chiropractic from National University of Health Sciences in Lombard, Illinois. She was a pre-med biology major student at YSU. She was the founding president of the American Medical Student Association (A.M.S.A.) chapter at her college. During her sophomore year, she went to the A.M.S.A. conference in Chicago. After returning to the university, she realized her passion was not traditional, allopathic medicine. She needed a new path and started researching other paths of medicine. She eventually decided on chiropractic medicine because chiropractic can help free people from pain and help them recover from injuries without drugs while preventing unnecessary surgeries. Chiropractic medicine can treat people of all ages and is a natural form of treatment. Chiropractors do more than adjusting the spine. They can treat many diseases and injuries including vertigo, arthritis, sciatica, herniated disc pain, and more.

She chose to attend National University because it is one of the oldest chiropractic colleges in the country and has a rich history among the field of chiropractic. There is a huge research base coming from the university, and she believes this was and still is one of the best chiropractic colleges in the country. National University of Health Sciences is a multidisciplinary university and has several programs including chiropractic, naturopathic, oriental medicine, and massage therapy. While attending chiropractic college, Dr. Edirisooriya felt she needed to learn more in order to be the best chiropractor she could be. She recognized her passion for acupuncture and enrolled in the program. She is certified in acupuncture and uses her knowledge to treat a variety of conditions such as headaches, anxiety, infertility, insomnia, smoking cessation, hair loss, and allergies.

Once she graduated from chiropractic college, she moved to Chandler, Arizona to escape the cold weather and to be closer to her family. She started as an associate chiropractor at a multidisciplinary practice in Chandler. After a year and a half, she left the practice to start her own. She started AcuChiro in Chandler in 2016 where she specializes in chiropractic, physiotherapy, and acupuncture. She has the following certifications: Graston Technique, Kinesio Taping, Motion Palpation Institute, and Mckenzie Diagnostic Technique. These are some of the most effective treatments for soft tissue injuries. Throughout her clinical and educational experience, she developed a focus on rehab-based chiropractic care in order to educate her patients and give them the tools they need to accomplish their goals. She has extensive experience with sports and sports injuries. She has treated many professional athletes including those who have competed in snowboarding, football, ice skating, soccer, and basketball.

Dr. Edirisooriya has the ability to individualize her treatment plans based on the specific concerns and the goals of each patient. She has had success with children, adults, athletes, and everyone in between. Dr. Edirisooriya looks forward to helping you achieve peak health and wellness through chiropractic, physiotherapy, and acupuncture.

When she is not treating patients, she spends her time traveling, watching sports, and volunteering for the Chandler Chamber of Commerce and her local Toastmasters chapter. She has appeared as a guest speaker for numerous local events to educate the public on the benefits of chiropractic and acupuncture. She is a guest contributor for the *SanTan Sun News* and *Gilbert Sun News* newspapers.

Her personal mission is to impact as many people as possible with the effectiveness of natural medicine. She is grateful that she is able to make a difference in the lives of the patients she treats.

About Sithari's Company
AcuChiro
Chiropractic Clinic
www.acuchiroaz.com

Do the Thing!

MICHAEL FRITZIUS
President

How I Got My Start

I'd been in software testing and test automation for a couple years as a consultant when I started thinking to myself, "Hm... I'll bet I could do this on my own." I had some people warn me away from it, saying "It's really hard to run your own business. You have to worry about insurance and all this other stuff. It's not worth it." And I'll admit, at the time, that did put me off a bit. But as the years went by, I kept thinking it was something I wanted to do.

One day a good friend of mine, a recruiter, was telling me about starting up an LLC. The advice was it's a good thing to just have; you can always fall back on it some, and in a way, it can mask employment gaps. Whatever it was that made me want to do it, I went ahead and filled out the info on the secretary of state website. All I had to do was push the button.

And one day, I got my termination notice from a client. They were letting contractors go. It wasn't anything personal, and they very graciously gave me a month's notice, but I was on the way out. That evening, I clicked the button and became a business.

It was odd, but my first client came almost immediately after I got my notice. I had called an old manager and told him what I was planning to do (this was before my notice), and right away, he jumped: "We actually need that kind of help. When can you start?" The timing was amazing.

My Advice to Aspiring Business Owners and Entrepreneurs

This may be the hardest thing you ever do. There will be times that you'll wish you never started. The allure of taking a comfortable salaried job is a real thing. People will think you're crazy. Heck, YOU will think you're crazy. But deep down, you'll hear the clarion call of whatever it is that keeps driving you forward, keeps making you stand up again every time you fall, and keeps reminding you of the reason why you started this crazy journey. It doesn't get easier; it just gets different. And if you know what I'm talking about, you know you can't ignore it because ignoring it is not an option. Do the thing.

About Michael

 I love software. I love it so much that I test it to make sure it's correct. I love that so much that I write automation to test it faster. And I love that so much that I teach other people how to automate their testing too. Companies and people are changing because of what we do.

Partnerships are being formed with other companies to increase how we can help. We're making a huge impact. I love that.

I also love my family. When I'm not slinging tech, I'm dadding four beautiful daughters and teaming-up with my wife to tackle the day-to-day of being a homeschool family. Every day is an opportunity to influence people in powerful ways, and I seek to honor the Lord in all that I do.

About Michael's Company
Arch DevOps
Custom Software Development, Websites, Software Testing, Automation, and Leadership
archdevops.com

Take Leaps of Faith

FLORENCE GASPARD
Speaker • Author • Success Coach

How I Got My Start

I grow up with parents who were entrepreneurs, and the bug was passed down to me. My dad was great with his hands and worked in construction and furniture designer and transitioned to working for himself in his mid-career. My mother always had her side gig as a merchant reselling home items to vendors and other clients as she worked her full-time job. Her side gig eventually became her full-time venture. Additionally, she got me started on my entrepreneurial journey when I was in middle school, selling lollipops to my peers at school. I continued selling into my high school years as I added various snacks to my inventory. I worked my snack business up until I was asked by our school administrators to stop selling on school grounds.

From there, I went on a hiatus, focusing on my studies and taking the traditional path of going to school so I could work in a career. Although, I took the traditional path, graduating with my degrees in the field of psychological related fields, I was still hearing the call from my entrepreneurial spirit to return to my roots. I worked as a therapist for a few years before and eventually transitioning to entrepreneurship full time. I utilized my schooling, studies, and experiences and merged them into my business practices.

Currently, I consult, coach, and train individuals, groups and organizations with meeting specific goals and outcomes. I take my love for educating and creating strategies to help others thrive in their spaces both personally and professionally. I am also an author; writing books provided me another outlet to share my messages and knowledge in order to reach more people. It's been a rewarding journey thus far, and I'm looking forward to what the future brings.

My Advice to Aspiring Business Owners and Entrepreneurs

My advice is to take leaps of faith towards fulfilling your dreams and believe in yourself that you can achieve whatever you desire while ensuring you adopt the right mindset, direction, and discipline. Also, some of us wait for validation from others to be okay with us pursuing our dreams, or we wait for things to be perfect before we start instead of taking action now with where we are. I say don't wait for others to give you permission, and there is no better time to start than now. Do something that moves you towards your goals no matter how small it appears. Grant yourself the permission and find your own way. There will be resources and people who are going to appear along the way to support you after you start the process. Take it upon yourself to be open to finding them. Once you are moving forward with pursuing your dreams, ideas or ideas, the universe will conspire to meet you where you are. Trust the process, and trust God.

About Florence

Florence Gaspard is an entrepreneur, professional speaker, corporate trainer, and author. She helps individuals, groups and businesses integrate efficient changes by offering programs and workshops, tools, and strategies that are simple and practical and that are designed to improve performance-driven results to meet their target goals and achieve the best outcomes. Additionally, Florence authored two well-received books to include her recent release, *I'm Unstoppable: A Guide to Transforming Your Life*, and her children's book, *Loving the Incredible Me*.

Florence travels nationally and internationally to expand her platform and reach a broader audience base. This also includes exposure on various media outlets and appearances on local and national radio stations, televised programs, and publications. Florence's mission is to help people elevate their mindsets, improve personally and professionally, and reach their goals. Join her movement in becoming unstoppable in your life and living the life you want.

About Florence's Company
Florence Gaspard
Life and Business Coaching and Consulting
www.florencegaspard.com

Do Your Research

CHANDRA GORE

Consultant • Publicist • Speaker • Author • Producer • Festival Founder

How I Got My Start

I was prompted and Inspired to start my business by my father who was a serial entrepreneur. He taught me that business ownership was the key to being free and to having unlimited earnings and your own schedule. I was so in awe of him that at nine, I "opened" up my own window washing and parking lot cleaning company so that I could show my dad I could do it.

I would later start accompanying my father while he worked his landscaping business and took over some of the lawns cut so I would have my own lawns to cut. I worked hard during the summers to earn as much money as I could to put towards my school clothes and to save.

I kept this motivation, even after having a career, by starting a baking and catering company, Sweet Simplicity Desserts. My company thrived with word of mouth referrals and a simple website before the addition of social media. I learned an important lesson that has stuck with me. Having a person-to-person connection was key to gaining referrals and interest in my company. When social media finally gained traction and kept growing, my business took off even more.

When my father got sick, with a heavy heart, I chose to close that business, and I then opened my business consulting firm a couple of years later. After the lessons learned in my previous business, I found that I had a knack for assisting others. Opening my firm allowed me to assist others with starting their businesses and understanding what was needed for success. As I worked with businesses, I began to see that they needed more reach to different audiences, and they needed to tell their stories of "why" and stories about their businesses, so I added public relations services to my firm. I found that I thrived in doing so by securing international and national news for some of my clients. When I saw that my comedian clients did not have perform-ance clips and photos, I opened up my production company to assist with capturing their acts and even began to produce my own events for them to perform at. In working within the comedy field, I saw there weren't many female producers or festivals headed by women, so I launched my own festival to provide a platform of my own to show-case the comics that were in the northern Virginia area. I feel that having multiple businesses keeps me on my toes and if, and when I am inspired to open another, then I will. I want to leave a legacy in honor of my father, and I want to create generational wealth for my children to ensure that their futures will be bright.

My Advice to Aspiring Business Owners and Entrepreneurs
The advice I would give someone who wants to start a business is to do your research, but do not put off working. While you are preparing

yourself to launch, begin working. You can start by creating a list of goals for your business. Look up the licensing and registration requirements for your business category in your county, state, and on the federal level. Consider your business name as well; check the abbreviation and different variations that would work. Keep in mind this is the first representation of your business so be creative. Consult with an accountant; this is an important factor as it determines how your business will operate. Having an accountant on board from the beginning of your business will also assist you with scaling and creating the best financial strategies to implement. This will also help you to determine the start-up costs and if a loan or grant is required. Trust me; this step is very important. Many entrepreneurs will go at it alone at this part. But my secret to success is networking. Network with those in the industry in which you are interested in working. You have to create a foundation that is solid, which includes finding others who are like minded and have been working in your field. You would be remiss if you did not speak to others who have been successful and who have had failures in their businesses. This can help you avoid any pitfalls that usually befall entrepreneurs at the beginning. This step can also help you narrow down a mentor should you choose to have one for your business.

About Chandra

Chandra Gore is a speaker, moderator, an author, and experienced entrepreneur who is the founder of multiple businesses. As a consultant and publicist, Chandra works with entrepreneurs to help them create foundations for success through her boutique success firm, Chandra Gore Consulting. She also heads a production company, SCM Productions, which produces live comedic events and an upcoming comedy series, "They Said What?!" The series will be launched strictly on Amazon. She has also launched the Accelerate Radio Network, an online radio station that provides a platform for those who want to have their social commentary heard. Her love for community support inspired her to create The Urban Flight Foundation to provide voter and other pertinent information to those who are seeking resources and assistance from other organizations. She heads the Greater Northern Virginia Comedy and Film Festival that is a yearly multi-day festival that showcases comedic performances. Witnessing the lack of support from her colleagues in public relations, she has partnered with a fellow publicist to create the PR Collective DC. An Horry County, South Carolina native, she now calls Stafford, Virginia her home.

About Chandra's Company

Chandra Gore Consulting
Consulting
www.chandragoreconsulting.com

Be Very Clear on WHY You Are Starting Your Business

DAMON GIVEHAND
Yoga & Health Mindset Coach • Happiness Catalyst

How I Got My Start

What drove me to eventually pick the entrepreneurial path and stick with it? Let's see ... In my previous life, I worked lots of jobs in a wide range of industries. Over time, as I grew, the following things became glaringly obvious and less tolerable until they became not tolerable at all.

The missions of the business organizations I worked for never aligned completely with my personal sense of purpose. Once the rubber hit the road, the core values of those businesses, no matter how good they might have appeared outwardly, failed to completely match my essence, which I was only able to figure out after I spent some time on the inside. Either something was out of alignment altogether, or there was always something missing that my soul yearned to do to full scale.

My time, and what I could do with my time, was unreasonably fettered, limited, and controlled. The number of hours I had to myself each day, to utilize at my discretion, were substantially hampered, if not impeded entirely. Additionally, the structure of my time from day to day was largely controlled or dictated by my job duties and designated work hours. And the amount of time I could take off from those jobs (despite being limited to a number of weeks per year) required the approval (permission) of those employers. Time is infinitely more valuable than money, and it became clear that my employers exercised greater ownership over my time than I did. I reached a point when I was no longer willing to accept that reality.

There was a definite ceiling on my earning potential as an employee. No matter how stellar an employee's performance might be and no matter how much of an asset that employee might prove to be for an organization, there is a limit to how much an employee can earn that will never add up to that person's true worth. I just had to accept and embrace that if I seek employment and accept that job when presented with an offer of employment, it is me who does not recognize my value. I had to learn that if I acquiesced to remain an employee, the company is not to blame and should not be viewed with contempt. In short, I began to recognize my own worth, and pursuing the entrepreneur's path was like putting my money where my mouth was and is.

The time eventually arrived when my feet were too big to fit the shoes of employment, and it was time for me to walk a new way. The experience I managed to accumulate, and the growth I'd undergone up to that point right before I decided to take the entrepreneur's path supplied me with all I needed to know to determine my heartfelt, soul-centered, and spirit-driven purpose. Thankfully, I didn't rush into entrepreneurship before I was truly ready, for if I had, there is a good chance that it would have been purely for better earnings and time freedom (which many tout as good enough for them, but those reasons often prove to be a seductive trap preventing people from actualizing their fullest potential), and not necessarily aligned with my true and ultimate purpose.

My Advice to Aspiring Business Owners and Entrepreneurs

My advice to the person who is beginning from scratch with little to no financial support and no lump sum of money to begin with is to be clear about why you are starting your business and pursuing an entrepreneurial path. Your why will determine if you are able to weather the storms you will undoubtedly encounter as you figure out the nuances of your unique venture. Without a clear why, it'll be easy to quit when the going gets tough ... and there will be times when things get tough.

Beginning with a clear why doesn't mean that your why will not transform and evolve over time, it most likely will. Change is inevitable as you get clearer, and with greater clarity your precision will increase, which will lead to greater success over time—and this can only happen with experience. With each new experience, there will be new lessons to learn, and if you know why you are engaged in your special kind of business, you will be eager to learn each new lesson. Being clear makes even the apparently negative experience a positive one, because the silver lining is always in the opportunity you have to learn something you did not know before. To say that with age comes wisdom isn't necessarily true, unless with your age comes experience from which you've been learning. (This means—if you want to speed things up a little—get off your butt and go create experiences for yourself, if you have to, that will allow you to learn the most for your benefit.)

That said, your why and your line of business should ultimately contribute to the highest quality of your life, which means Happiness (with a capital H). If you are not happy at the end of the day, what's the point of such business? So, as much as possible, based on the amount of experience you've gained up to this point in your life, make sure that your business and/or entrepreneurial pursuits are in total agreement with your heart, soul, spirit, and health; as all these combined comprise your unique compass that'll orient you toward Happiness and your ultimate purpose in life (which is what you are here to ultimately fulfill).

As developer and cocreator of the R.I.C.H. Life™ philosophy and The 12 Radical Intentions™ (R.I.C.H. is an acronym for radically intent on cultivating happiness), there are several questions I like to ask folks (who are looking to go into business for themselves) to explore in depth. If you had a billion dollars (meaning lack of finances posed no object or impediment, and therefore couldn't be used as an excuse), how would you live your life day to day that would bring you the greatest joy and help you feel totally whole? What would you learn and possibly become an expert in? Where would your personal, intrinsic interests tend to concentrate? What have you always wanted to be great at? What do you want your eulogy to read? Write out your (daily, weekly, monthly, and/or yearly) dream routine for living your best, most fulfilled life, including travel, and the reasons for wanting to visit. Hold nothing back and let your imagination run completely wild with how your life would look if you could have it any way you want. Write out the chapters of your life that you haven't lived yet. Be as detailed and vivid as possible.

Pull out a journal and write down as much as you can that pours out of your heart onto the page without editing. Don't worry about writing things down perfectly or saying what you think smart people say. Speak your heart and give voice to your soul and spirit without letting your head get in the way. What you write from this pure inner place will provide you with genuine fodder from which you will be able to extrapolate your why and begin to gain the clarity you need to go all the way.

About Damon

In 2015, Damon Givehand formulated an acronym for R.I.C.H., which stands for radically intent on cultivating happiness. He went on to cocreate and develop the R.I.C.H. Life™ philosophy and The 12 Radicals Intentions™ with his wife Kiala. In addition, Damon is the author of *Optimum Health Mindset (OHM): How to Think to Undo Fat, Maximize Your Vitality, and Never Get Sick Again* and *YOGA, Truth, and The Real Fountain of Youth.* For at least the past eighteen years, Damon has been on a quest to learn what's fundamentally necessary to heal physically and how to live the highest quality life possible, and yoga has been integral to his path.

Damon was introduced to yoga for the first time just after the turn of the millennium, and from 2006 to 2007, he and Kiala attended and completed his first yoga teacher training, which consisted of 200 hours in Ashtanga Yoga/Vinyasa Flow at Bliss Yoga in Jacksonville, Florida. Five years later, from 2010 to 2012, he completed a 500-hour teacher training program in Viniyoga at the Healing Yoga Foundation in San Francisco, California. At the time of this publication, he's a student with Yoga Well Institute in an advanced 1,000-hour training and is on track to becoming an internationally certified yoga therapist.

Damon combines all he knows about yoga, healing, cultivating life conditions that lead to Happiness (with a capital H), and the spectrum of yoga tools beyond the mat into unique and powerful practices that help people transform in the greatest ways at the deepest levels.

About Damon's Company
Healing Arts Creative Studio
Health, Wellness, and Whole Life Improvement
healingartscreativestudio.com
damongivehand.com

Learn to Listen to the Whispers of Your Heart

KIALA GIVEHAND, MFA, EdS.
Life Alchemist • Happiness Catalyst

How I Got My Start

Growing up I always heard people talk about "being called." As a younger woman, I thought that only applied to being called to minister or to become a nun. I had no idea that one could be called to start a business. But when I kept waking up in the middle of the night with ideas for businesses that I could start, it finally made sense to me. I was being called to start a business.

And so, I did. The first one was semi-successful. I made some money, but barely enough to claim on my taxes. And so, I did it again. The second business was amazing, and I had lots of success to the point where I sold my curriculum to a similar, but much larger, company for a nice profit. After the sale, I still felt the tug each night to revisit my list of business ideas. And so, I did it again, and again, until I figured out what was working for me and what was not. I kept starting over until I found a rhythm to my work and found the kind of work that didn't feel like work.

Yes! You can do what you love and get paid for it. You can wake up every single day and do the things that bring you joy and live a comfortable financial life. Don't get me wrong, working for yourself is going to be Work (with a capital "W"), but that doesn't mean it can't also be Fun (with a capital "F").

I started my business because I felt the call to work for myself and on my own terms. In my mid-twenties, I felt stifled working for others even though that is how I was taught. I was taught that to achieve the American dream one must work for others. Ideally, they would pay you handsomely and you would have a 401(k) and these things would allow you to buy a house, a car, and a life that would make it possible for you to travel and take vacations multiple times a year, and eventually retire to a life of leisure and certainty. A job was supposed to be the promise of a great life. But as a full-time teacher in the public school system, that seemed well out of reach as I was struggling from paycheck to paycheck and unable to save money or live the life of my dreams. Seriously, I was still calling home for help from my mother during my first three years of teaching.

I loved teaching but I felt oppressed by the logistics of the job, by having to grade hundreds of papers a year, by attending countless meetings, and by dealing with never-ending discipline problems of students who were ill-equipped for the structure of school. I loved my students and I did not want to continue to do the kind of work that made me feel without purpose and made me resent the people I was charged with guiding and inspiring. I wanted to do work that was meaningful to me and to those I was helping. I wanted to work with people who self-selected my products and services. And so, I found myself in search of other ways to make money and to get free of the traditional nine-to-five teaching job.

Thank goodness that I now get to do exactly that—work with women who want to work with me, create products that people want to purchase, and teach classes that are filled with purpose and passion for people who want to attend. But the truth is, I didn't have a lot of examples in my life of people who had done what I was hoping to do. I didn't understand where to begin or what it was supposed to look like. I only knew of traditional jobs and careers. I knew that I didn't want someone else to define my worth. I didn't want someone else to say that the hours of time and energy I give are worth X number of dollars.

I wanted time freedom, location freedom, and most important, I wanted financial freedom. I wanted to travel more and do the things I was passionate about. And so with a whole lot of fear in my heart and mind, I started that first business; the second business; and the third, fourth, and fifth businesses; which all led me down a path of purpose and divine destiny. I heeded the call. I listened to my heart and with each business I did the work that felt, at the time, in alignment with a higher calling.

Yes, there were times when I had to take a regular gig to make ends meet and pay my bills. But it was a small sacrifice for what I knew the payoff would eventually be. I had moments of self-doubt and lots of rejections, false starts, missteps, and flat-out failures. Each one felt like an opportunity to reassess and, if necessary, begin anew.

I knew by the fourth business that what was going to bring me ultimate joy was to do it my way. To revise what others had done before me in the online teaching and coaching industry and do what felt good and right in my heart. I knew that I would need to rely on my own inner wisdom and guidance to create the kind of business that I wanted to wake up and do every single day. It took me years (that doesn't mean it will take you years), several thousand dollars, and lots of revisions to figure out exactly what I was being called to do and in what way I was being called to do it.

It was always teaching. I hadn't planned on becoming a teacher when I went off to college at 17. I was sure I was going to be a computer programmer who sat behind a desk with limited human contact on a daily basis. I was going to be behind the scenes, coding and creating amazing programs and software for people to use in their work and personal lives. But I was called to teaching in my third year of college and I've been on that path ever since. And I don't regret a single moment of this journey. All the classes, lessons, workshops, and conferences I've attended for the past twenty-plus years have led me to the work I do today. The work I cherish. The work I was called to do.

So, here's where I tell you that I'm not trying to make it sound easy, and also in the same sentence tell you that it's absolutely that easy. Just decide that you are going to follow your heart. It's that simple. The hard part, the real work, is learning to listen to those callings. It has been the number-one skill that increased my success and helped me achieve my goals much faster. And yes, learning to hear our own heart's whispers is a skill we must train ourselves to do well. It's something that is often taught out of us or forgotten. It's something we have to hone, sharpen, and strengthen. And once we do, we must listen and unapologetically follow the sound of our own inner voice.

My Advice to Aspiring Business Owners and Entrepreneurs

My advice to those just starting or those starting over is this. "Embrace fear and welcome failure, then simply begin." Don't wait to start. I have found, after working with hundreds of women that the only thing holding them back is fear. The fear of not getting it perfect, the fear that you don't have enough time, the fear that you don't have enough money to start a business, the fear that no one will like your idea or take you seriously, the fear that you have not taken the right courses or earned the right degrees, the fear that you are not worthy of success, the fear that others will think you're weird or strange for wanting to start your own business, the fear of not having financial security, the fear of losing your 401(k), the fear of not being able to put food on the table, the fear of not being able to pay your bills, the fear of success, and on and on. I could list a thousand fears that will surface as soon as you decide to begin. Accept them as your inner child and inner wisdom trying to protect you. Embrace the fear as something that directs you toward your dreams. See your failures as proof that you are trying something new, something different, and something worthy.

Do things that will help you cultivate a positive and nurturing relationship with your inner voice. Here are some suggestions: daily journaling, silent meditation, yoga, intuitive art, listing what your heart most wants then doing your best to give yourself those things, and finding spaces where you can speak your dreams out loud. That last one is powerful because it asks you to find others who can share in the weaving of your dream.

This is the work I do for women, I create spaces where they can speak their dreams out loud to others who will hold their dreams as sacred and necessary to our world. This is not something to take lightly or to give to just anyone. Find a coach or mentor who believes in you and understands the power of dreaming and speaking those dreams out loud. And make sure they also give you room to fail, to forget, to falter, and to eventually celebrate. All these things are important to the work of being a thriving business owner. When you learn to listen to the whispers of your heart, you will learn how to own your dreams and become radically intent on seeing them come true. This process is the journey.

About Kiala

Kiala Givehand is a published poet, bookbinder, teacher and workshop leader, fountain pen collector, and radical nomad. She believes in surrounding herself with ordinary humans who live extraordinary lives, gathering with people who allow her to laugh and love uncontrollably, and living a life intent on cultivating happiness. Kiala is a double Capricorn and an ambivert who grew up on the Gulf Coast of Florida, where she learned to appreciate and respect hurricanes; humidity; and the transformational powers of the sun; the transformational powers of the sun, the moon, and the ocean. She holds six academic degrees in various subjects from various universities, but the one she cherishes most is her Master of Fine Arts in creative writing and poetry from Mills College, where she fell in love with book art.

In her day-to-day life, Kiala empowers women to live more fully and intentionally. She guides women who want to liberate their creativity, explore deep inner work, experience radical transformation, and create a life filled with passion and purpose. In her professional speaking life, Kiala has delivered more than five hundred talks, speeches, presentations, and trainings to thousands of people around the world. Her signature talks include "Passion and Purpose: The Introverts Guide to Engagement," "Strategize and Thrive: Twelve Ways to Live a Life Radically Intent on Cultivating Happiness," and "Creative Empowerment: The Power of Intuition and Intention."

Kiala's writing has appeared in *Brush Magazine, Mabel Magazine, Calyx: A Journal of Literature by Women, Cave Canem Anthology XIII,* Eleven Eleven, Jacket 2, the Bella Vista Art Gallery, and the Campanil. She is a SoulCollage® facilitator, a Cave Canem fellow, a Voices of Our Nations (VONA) alum, and a member of Delta Sigma Theta Sorority, Inc. Kiala obsessively studies astrology, sacred geometry, mandalas, and other ancient intuitive systems as a way to know herself more fully and compassionately. Through online courses and in-person retreats/workshops, she teaches women all over the world how to find what makes them happy and pursue it without regrets.

About Kiala's Company

Healing Arts Creative Studio

Health, Wellness, and Whole Life Improvement

http://kialagivehand.com

Know Your Values

JACQUELINE GRIFFIN
CEO • Founder

How I Got My Start

On this journey called life, I have learned many things that have shaped me to be the person I am today. Five areas of my life that demanded my attention and prompted an opportunity for growth and ways I would not have imagined are spiritual centeredness, emotional balance, social connections, physical health, and financial stability. Each one of these areas was a struggle for me throughout my life. I had to do some hard work in each area that was not always pleasant or embraced. I had to work on self-awareness, self-confidence, exploring and embracing my feelings and emotions, maintaining a healthy lifestyle through all the stressors, finding balance and beauty in developing and sustaining long-term relationships/friendships, and facing the ugly fact of my financial situation of being broke.

After years of working as a spiritual counselor, I realize I wanted to share my journey—my story of being self-sufficient, self-motivated, and self-driven to change the direction of my life. I knew there were other women, especially career women, who have worked all their lives to climb the ladder of success while other areas were unfulfilled. In knowing this, I became a certified life coach and started my coaching business called H.O.A.L. Living, Healing On All Levels L.L.C. This organization is for career women who need balance in their lives, becoming whole on all levels possible to continue to be the phenomenal women they are. H.O.A.L. Living provides one-on-one coaching, group sessions for personal growth, webinars, and social gatherings. Our mission is to motivate, inspire, and encourage you to live a life of wholeness on every level possible. Our vision is to become a world-class life coaching organization, equipping women with cutting-edge tools to live a life of balance on every level imaginable.

My Advice to Aspiring Business Owners and Entrepreneurs

In starting my business, I knew it was vital for me to have alignment. What do I mean by alignment? I'm glad you ask. Who you are and what you do should always be in alignment with your value system. I believe the values you hold and the principles by which you live are the core parts of who you are, and if you start a business, the foundation of the business centers around your core value system. If I believe in being authentic and transparent, then the principles I create in my business should be building off of authenticity and transparency. In starting your business, knowing what values are essential to you and incorporating them in your business will always keep you aligned with the mission and vision.

About Jacqueline

Too often, we as human beings forget or lose sight of why we are here. Life is too short not to celebrate every day. Good or bad, experiences bring weight that can overload our mental and physical well-being. With over twenty years of providing spiritual and emotional care, Jacqueline Griffin is the CEO and founder of H.O.A.L. Living, Healing On All Levels, LLC. Jacqueline Griffin and H.O.A.L. Living are about encouraging you to live the whole life you deserve on all levels.

Jacqueline is the youngest daughter of Catherine and James White. Jacqueline spent most of her younger years struggling with her self-identity and low self-esteem. She never allowed her lack of confidence stop her in pursuing her education and other career goals; she was determined to do something different with her life than what she grew up around. Jacqueline had many obstacles to overcome, and with the help of God and her tenacity, she beat the odds every time. She was a first-generation college graduate, and years later, she pursued her graduate degrees. Life always presented itself with many challenges for Jacqueline, and she faced every challenge with boldness and courage as she grew older and embraced the fulness of who she was becoming. Jacqueline felt a strong call on her life to preach and help people discover their purpose-given gifts and embrace their beauty from the inside.

Jacqueline started her spiritual journey as a minister in 1998 and was ordained as an elder in the Pentecostal church in 2005. In 2001,

Jacqueline began seminary at Bethel College and graduated with two master's in theology and education. Jacqueline Griffin served in the Army Reserve during the Operation of Desert Shield/Storm, resigned, and re-enlisted in 2003 until 2007 in the National Guard as an officer in the role of a chaplain. Jacqueline received the National Defense Service Medal and Army Service Ribbon for her service during the Desert Storm. Jacqueline has enjoyed her time serving and training the most loyal, respectful, honorable, and courageous group of men and women—our soldiers. While in the military, she participated in reintegrating our soldiers back into day-to-day living after deployment to fight the war on terrorism. She was a certified trainer in The Prevention and Relationship Enhancement Program (PREP) and certified trainer in Applied Suicide Intervention Skills Training (ASIST). She has acquired other skills from critical incident stress management, pastoral crisis intervention, and psychological first aid, to name a few, that equipped her to help those who were emotionally and spiritually challenged.

Jacqueline has always enjoyed serving the hurt and wounded and walking alongside those who find themselves in spiritual or emotional distress. Once she resigned from the military, Jacqueline continued to pursue her career as a civilian chaplain working in hospitals, nursing homes, and hospice. Jacqueline is always growing and enjoys empowering people to become the "best you possible." She has enjoyed her time serving our soldiers and now serving others as they transition to their next place in life.

Jacqueline Griffin has assisted many people in navigating through the assortment of waves and hardships life generates. Jacqueline endured hardships, including divorce, loss of loved ones, financial struggles, questions of faith, and health issues. Jacqueline pushed through and found herself working through many areas of her life to overcome the challenges and strive for wholeness every day. In doing her work on becoming whole, she launched her coaching business to help other women who are struggling with the balance of life. Committed to her craft, Jacqueline earned her certification as a life coach. Having already obtained her board certification as a chaplain, Jacqueline continues to grow as she embodies the fullness of who she is becoming through her life journey.

Jacqueline's goal is to create a non-judgmental space for women to feel inspired and motivated as they strive to live balanced and whole lives. Beginning with a discovery session, Jacqueline takes her clients on a magnificent eight-session journey towards self-discovery and personal development. Simple discussions enable the client to feel safe while providing the details for Jacqueline to work through to offer insight. At www.hoallifecoach.com, people can view the many incredible ways Jacqueline can help you on your journey. From spiritual, physical, emotional, and financial quests, Jacqueline has the tools and experience to open new doors for her clients. Living H.O.A.L. is my goal; how about you?

About Jacqueline's Company
H.O.A.L. Living, Healing On All Levels, LLC
Coaching Business
www.hoallifecoach.com

Follow the Nudge ...
Don't Wait to Get Started

MOLIKA GUPTA

Transformational Coach • Public Speaker • Patent Licensing
Consultant

How I Got My Start

My journey to start my business was not a straightforward path. It
really was not even a path. It happened to me in my rock bottom
moments.

I come from an Asian background, and if you know anything about
growing in a Southeast Asian home, earning advanced degrees and
getting a stable corporate job is pretty much the only option.

Growing up, I was always that person whose friends used to call to
get advice and share their stories. I always was a great listener, very
intuitive, and ready to share my advice. The option to explore my
passions never occurred to me. I was preparing myself to study
medicine and become a doctor. Life had completely different plans,
and instead, I became a patent associate in a law firm.

I got married to my childhood friend and relocated to the USA. Yes, I did pack my entire life in a red American Tourister bag and moved halfway across the globe. I always had this nudge to start something of my own, but I was on this corporate treadmill.

So, after marriage, I went up to earn my second master's degree from Chicago while braving the icy cold commute. February of 2014 was one of the most brutal winters Chicago has ever seen and it also became my first winter in States. I then immediately got hired by a Chicago downtown-based corporate company to work for its patent department. I still remember enjoying views of Willis Tower from my desk on the thirteenth floor while having my morning coffee.

The nudges of starting something of my own had become non-existent by now. I was running full speed ahead on my ambitious career train. The American dream as an immigrant is a dream that many see but very few fulfill it. I was the one who was living and breathing that dream.

Until one day things changed. Life changed. I changed. Things happened, and I had to leave my position and change my visa status to a non-working spousal visa. The immigration journey never bothered me until that point.

During the twelve months that followed, I lost myself. I went from dressing sharp in my CK blue pantsuits to not even feeling motivated to take a bath. I kept asking myself "Why me? What's next from here? Where do I go from here?" As I was hitting rock bottom in all areas of life, an idea sparked inside of me to write a memoir. I kept toying with that idea for almost a year. Then an opportunity presented itself, and I submitted my first chapter to an authoring program. The host of that program called my name on the live webinar and said I can't wait for your book to hit bookshelves. That really was the first time in years, that old nudge of starting something of my own came back. I knew I had to explore this further.

I attended countless webinars and courses on book writing programs, but I couldn't finish it. There was something that I felt I needed to explore further.

With the intent to connect with my audience, I started my online community, a Facebook group, called Rewrite Your Story that's a community for ex-pat spouses to share and connect. I still remember the joy when my group hit one hundred members. That group really became the starting point for my entrepreneurial journey.

Over the course of growing the group, I realized that I have a passion for speaking, writing, and coaching. The cherry on the top was members inside the group were listening to me. As the group grew, I discovered my purpose. I discovered myself again, and the question "Why me?" stopped bothering me.

Today, the group has grown to 2.5 thousand ex-pats and immigrant spouses from all over the world, I have bylines in publications like Detroit News, I have been a guest speaker on several podcasts, I have coached many women to tap into their power and make a comeback in career and life. Early this April, I also launched my podcast, The C Factor, where I interviewed thirteen ex-pat women from eleven countries in lockdown.

Honestly, I didn't start my business; my business restarted me. It gave me my purpose and the reason to share my story with someone like you.

Follow the nudge. Life is taking you somewhere. Trust it.

My Advice to Aspiring Business Owners and Entrepreneurs

The best expert you can ever consult is yourself. Don't let an over pouring of business information consume you. The fact that you are even having the courage to start your business is the evidence that you are meant to be on this path. Trust that spark—that little voice that brought you to be right here in this moment, reading this book. Once you start trusting the nudges—those nagging ideas that don't seem to leave you—keep believing that there is something bigger than yourself that is propelling you.

Don't wait to get started. Start with what you have in the now. Trust those perfect websites, the pipeline of clients, and the millions of dollars, media are on their way. For now, start with what you have and where you are in the now.

Take imperfect actions. Make progress over perfect actions. The majority of people wait to get started. The secret to success is to get started even when you don't have all the steps mapped out.

Put yourself out there on Facebook Lives, videos, webinars even when you are still trying to figure out who is your ideal client. No single book, course, or mentor can map out all the steps from start to finish for you to build a perfect business.

They can give you the nuggets, the crumbs to all the ideas that can hold you accountable. It's your job to run with those ideas, learnings, and advice and to carve your path and build your business. The people you are called to serve are unique to you and can be served only by you. To make you see my point, take for instance readers of Harry Potter. There are many fiction books available out there, but JK Rowling was called to serve the readers that were meant to read her writing. You must find your readers—clients, who are meant to be served by you.

Here is the cool part: they don't care how perfect you are or how polished is your bio or how great your website looks. All they care about is that you have the solution to the problem that they have, and you can give them that solution.

Don't delay your start because your customers are waiting for you to show up.

About Molika

Molika Gupta is a transformational coach, speaker, and author who is on a mission to catalyze women, especially expat spouses (women who relocated to a new country for marriage, career, or love), to make a comeback in career and life, stop playing small and go for opportunities in the workplace, and step in their power in personal lives.

Molika is also a patent licensing expert and is a double master's degree holder in biotechnology and patent management from

Chicago Kent College of Law, the second oldest law school in the state of Illinois, and she has worked with Fortune 500 American companies.

Molika also speaks on embracing uncertainty and victory through her story as an ex-pat woman of color and has been a guest on several podcasts including Becker Group Women's Leadership podcast, [1]Rorashach Your Reality, [2]And Then Suddenly, and online summits on topics including women rebirth.

Molika is also the host of the podcast [3] [4] [5]The C Factor, an upbeat podcast where she connected with sixteen women professionals from eleven countries in lockdown to find joy and connection amidst the 2020 coronavirus pandemic.

She also has bylines in publications such as *The Detroit News*, PBS, and Fast Company.

Molika is on the mission to catalyze ten thousand ex-pat women by 2025 to rewrite their stories, tap into the version they have become after their international move, and make a comeback in career and life with a bang.

Molika lives with her family in the lush green suburbs of Detroit, USA. She is addicted to drinking Indian ginger tea; loves reading; can spend her entire life in the city of Chicago; and when not doing above, she is practicing counts in training to become a Bollywood dance coach.

About Molika's Company

Coaching and Speaking
https://bit.ly/2T6AdHw

[1]www.rorschachyourreality.com/podcasts/rewrite-your-story-guest-molika-gupta
[2]www.stitcher.com/podcast/angela-santillo/and-then-suddenly/e/63673093
[3]https://anchor.fm/molika
[4]https://podcasts.apple.com/us/podcast/the-c-factor/id1507818494
[5]https://spoti.fi/2yoYkes

Narrow Down, Focus, and Craft a Plan

KELLY HALE
Author • Christian Financial Coach • Non-Practicing Certified Public Accountant

How I Got My Start

Never ever did I think that the most fun part of my business would be related to art. In seventh grade, I was very glad art was graded on effort instead of ability. My effort was extremely high, but my ability to sketch, draw, or paint was sorely lacking.

At about the same time, my parents purchased their first computer. I devoured all the training I could find on this machine from word processing to graphics. I taught myself to create flyers, posters, and websites before I ever knew what the term "graphic design" meant. Apparently, the missing piece in all my art classes was a mouse, keyboard, and CPU!

In college, I majored in computer science and communication studies. One of my first jobs after college was working in marketing for a nationwide agricultural publication. I loved the opportunity to combine my farm and ranch background with computers and design. My role was production-focused and fast-paced. I was learning new applications and graphic design techniques at a staggering pace, and I could not get enough.

Family considerations prompted a move from a metropolitan area back home to Nebraska. I began my master's degree program in accounting and transitioned to doing tax accountant work. I'm blessed to have multiple passions, and accounting fit the bill with technology demands, technical tax training, and being able to work with people.

I also began to design a few websites for local friends and family businesses, and that is when our company, Upward Designs, LLC, was born. Our company name came from always trying to help our customers move their business upward and onward.

Website design helped relax my brain after challenging days of trying to decode tax regulations or spending six to seven hours on the phone during the busy season. I invested in many different classes to continue learning about website coding, design, and scripting.

One of the classes taught how to create and market adult coloring books. At the time of taking the class, I began designing coloring pages for the book, and my daughters noticed what I was working on and asked to help "test" out the coloring pages themselves. After all, if they could color the pages at ages three and twelve, then they would be appropriate for all ages!

I finished about fifteen pages for the book and then took a break to pursue other opportunities. A few months later, my oldest daughter asked when I would finish the book. I received that question as inspiration to finish the book and get it published as quickly as possible. And now, I'm a published author on Amazon, and I've had the chance to gift several copies of the book to family members.

It took me a while to realize that computer art was not inferior to work done by pencil, paint, or other media. Although I'm unlikely to pick up a paintbrush anytime soon, I've stepped boldly into the world of coloring books. And this is just the beginning of our online publishing ventures. I can't wait to see what the future will bring.

My Advice to Aspiring Business Owners and Entrepreneurs

Starting a business is often a completely overwhelming process. Many people shut down before they ever start because they can't isolate a single idea as a starting point. Or they get distracted by other ideas that pull their attention away from starting something.

Starting a business usually involves a lot of learning. For some people, the big learning curve comes on the administrative side. For others, there might be a steep curve around industry regulations, contracts, or negotiation.

My best advice to someone starting a business is to narrow down your idea as quickly as possible, and focus on a single product or service when you first get started. Then craft a plan for all the startup paperwork and licenses while hiring professionals to help with the more complex tasks.

Don't skimp on marketing. Don't blow your startup capital either. You absolutely must get your product or service in front of potential customers, and good marketing will set your new business up for success from the start.

My accountant background is screaming at me to mention cash flow. Startup businesses require a lot of financial and time investment. Doing a cash flow projection as soon as possible can help identify financial weaknesses.

The saying "cash makes the world go 'round" will never be truer than when your new business is trying to generate enough cash to cover operating expenses at the beginning. Correcting cash flow deficiencies early in the startup phase will help the stability of the business every step of the way.

About Kelly

Kelly Hale is a published author, Christian financial coach, and a non-practicing Certified Public Accountant. She is an avid fan of Nebraska Husker volleyball, learned to speed read in a one-room elementary schoolhouse, and loves to gather with friends and family.

She and her husband own a web design, consulting, and online publishing business called Upward Designs, LLC. They are blessed to reside in Nebraska with three beautiful daughters who keep them on their toes.

About Kelly's Company

Upward Designs LLC

Online publishing, website design and consulting

www.upwarddesigns.com

Don't Give Up: Dream It, Then Do It

CLINTON HARRIS

CEO • Life Progression Expert • Best-Selling Author • Keynote Speaker

How I Got My Start

In my eyes, entrepreneurship was the ability to NOT DO so many things. Yes, you read that correctly. It was the pathway to NOT be held to the proverbial "9-to-5" schedule. It was the pathway to NOT be held to the critique and evaluation of a managerial superior. It was the ability to NOT be limited by the shackles found in corporate America, exonerating myself from the timecards, vacation limits, and corporate stiction set forth by others.

Yes, these were thoughts that came to mind after I entered the corporate arena, but if the truth be told, they were not the only catalysts nor were they the most prominent reasons for my decision.

I started my own business for multiple reasons. Simply put, I sought freedom—freedom to live, freedom to exist, and freedom to thrive but on my terms. I wanted to bring passion to the vision I had created of what my life should be. I wanted to create the life and the lifestyle I envisioned. Working for others does not always allow one the ability to live out his/her dreams. Most people don't have the ability to take the vacation they want or to buy the dream home that they've always perceived or the car that they've always desired to be at the helm of. Yes, these are all material things that flashed through my mind for a moment, but they turned out to not be MY reason although they are attractive prospects. My reason was much deeper, and that's evident in the types of businesses I chose to create.

I became an entrepreneur because I wanted to use my business aspirations to build something special. I wanted to build a brand that was synonymous with multiple words directly related to the word inspiration. I wanted to build a coaching firm that helped people overcome their root problems in order to use those hurdles as staircases towards their goals. I wanted to build a speaking platform that would allow me to relay my story and purvey my message to a global audience. These goals may very well help me entertain the fleeting thoughts of gaining those material possessions that some seek, including the material possessions in my mind, but my primary objective was to help those that are in need of some form of help via platforms that are accessible 24/7. In a nutshell, I started my business out of the desire to help others.

My Advice to Aspiring Business Owners and Entrepreneurs

The first piece of advice I would lend to anyone considering becoming an entrepreneur is simple, yet crucial. Learn the definition of what an entrepreneur truly is. I mean literally pick up a dictionary and read the definition verbatim, then allow it to soak in. The fact of the matter is, being an entrepreneur isn't always a walk in the park, it's not easy. One has to make a great deal of sacrifices to make their business a success in most cases. Usually it involves extended hours; a long-term investment of time, money and energy; less time at home with family and friends; and a lot of coffee! These are the by-products of a business that a dictionary source's definition cannot possibly communicate. The flip side to the coin is the positive side that definitely overshadows the negative aspects of entrepreneurship. This is the side of the coin where dreams come to fruition and goals are tangibly realized.

The next piece of advice is to create a solid blueprint. Moving forward without a plan is entrepreneurial suicide. First, Identify your target audience. Research similar business types, and find the one you are most comfortable with, then tweak it to fit your needs and the needs of your future customer base. Take time to brainstorm it, write it down, and organize it. Yes, even if you take these steps, it may not always work initially, and it may take some time to find a method, format, or product that does work for you, but don't give up.

The bottom line is this, entrepreneurship is freedom—your freedom to bring to fruition and express your hopes, aspirations, and goals by building your dream into a functioning reality. Don't sit on the sideline always saying "I should;" step onto the field and say "I did." If it's worth taking the time to dream it, then it's worth taking the time to build it. After all, are you not worth your own time?

About Clinton

Clinton Harris is a personal development expert, life progression coach, entrepreneur, keynote motivational speaker, and #1 best-selling author. He has worked with many well-respected experts in his field. Working in organizational leadership, in educational institutions, and with families and the military, he has served to help people all over the world for over a decade.

Clinton is the founder and CEO of Clinton Harris Coaching (CHC) and traverses the globe speaking his story at conventions, corporate events, and charitable organizations. He is currently involved with global corporations speaking for the benefit of their employees and with individuals coaching them beyond their internal and external hurdles in life. Multiple solo book projects are on the horizon for him as well as book compilation projects worldwide.

About Clinton's Company
Clinton Harris Coaching
Speaking/Coaching
www.clintonharriscoaching.com

Learn to Self-Cultivate and Self-Develop

MARCUS HINSCHBERGER
Sensei

How I Got My Start

I started Tokon Martial Arts with my wife, Christina, in 2012 with the birth of my first son, Takeo. My wife and I both come from families with a martial arts background, and we knew that some lessons for life are best taught through and within traditional martial arts. In fact, I believe that martial arts might be the best teaching tool to overcome fear, anxiety, and depression on one side while teaching commitment, focus, perseverance, self-cultivation, and self-realization on the other side.

Knowing about those hidden secrets and lessons, we wanted to ensure our son would learn and benefit from those lessons as well.

My Advice to Aspiring Business Owners and Entrepreneurs

My advice to anyone is to pick up a traditional (Japanese) martial art not only to learn the life-skill of self-defense but also to learn to self-cultivate and self-develop. Martial arts are not for children only but are for people of any age. Traditional martial arts are a great way to work out the full body (mind, body, AND SOUL), to help slow down (or even prevent) age-related diseases and decline and are also an activity that is sustainable into very old age.

The most important lesson one can learn from martial arts training is the confrontation with one's fears, doubts, hesitations, and personal shortcomings. This is not only extremely helpful to fight off anxiety and depression but essential for one's professional and self-development. Combine that with the other benefits, the student learns such a disciple, focus, perseverance, and commitment one gets a compelling package, and THE best activity one can do.

About Marcus

Sensei Marcus Hinschberger is a sixth-degree black belt with the International KarateCoaching Federation and a fifth-degree black belt with the Japan Karate Association (JKA). He is the founder of www.karatecoaching.com, which is the world's most comprehensive website.

Sensei Marcus started learning karate in 1990 and was directly mentored by senior Shotokan Karate instructors from Japan. He has participated in various national and international karate championships and was ranked as a Top-3 DJKB Shotokan Karate fighter in

2000 before coming to the United States from his homeland Germany.

The strong Japanese influence is still evident in his fighting spirit and warrior (budoka) mindset. Sensei Marcus has taught karate to numerous students and athletes around the world, helping them attain success in life, business, and competitions worldwide. As a personal trainer and athletic performance coach, he fuses the traditional Japanese training and values of karate-do with modern training techniques. Sensei Marcus is the owner of Tokon Martial Arts in Natomas, Sacramento, California where he teaches traditional karate and martial arts.

Sensei Marcus Hinschberger also runs a development training for industry leaders, entrepreneurs, and managers. This is known as Taitoku training, and it is beneficial for self-transformation, team training, and organizational leadership. Taitoku is a coaching company for Fortune 500 companies and other corporations that want to expand their market size.

About Marcus's Company
Tokon Martial Arts & Taitoku Training
Coaching and Martial Arts
www.TaitokuTraining.com
www.TokonSacramento.com

Dream It, Build It, Innovate It, and Deliver It Above Expectations

ERIC HOLTZ
Founder • Owner

How I Got My Start

Every business that I have ever started always began with a solution to a problem or something that I thought was a problem, need, or desire. I would tinker with it to find a better way, a better mousetrap, or a different angle or approach to solve a problem or to provide something that someone wanted or needed.

At some point in this journey and excitement, I would become passionate about the subject if I wasn't already. Once it made sense and was clearly apparent—and sometimes not so apparent—I would be prompted by the little business angel and devil perched on my shoulder to dive in, commence operations, and embark on a new business venture and vision.

The fact is that many ventures started by successful and not so successful businesspeople that end in failure. In reality, failure is not failure until you give up—even if it is a new venture, a new day, or another direction because failure is nothing more than a temporary lack of success.

You see, there is no such thing as true failure because every failure opens the door to another opportunity of success.

My desire to start my business has always been about helping someone else be successful in achieving a goal, solving a problem, or satisfying a need or want, opening the next door to success.

In conclusion, there are only three things that really matter in the world in which we live today –

Our belief system, humanity, and the earth. Nothing else really matters!

It is without hesitation and unequivocally that I can state that these three things are supported through dividends and through philanthropic and eco-centric projects.

The core solution to creating and sustaining dividends and philanthropic and eco-centric projects is through profit and surplus revenue.

I believe every business and organization has a unique profit and surplus revenue equation. My mission is solving that equation through custom-designed solutions.

It is, after all, about a vision to solve a big problem, helping others open the next door to success, and believing that we can make the world a better place through profit and surplus revenue.

That is why I started BusinessProfit2.2.

My Advice to Aspiring Business Owners and Entrepreneurs

I must cheat and bend the rules as one single piece of advice is not enough to start and succeed in business!

But... let us follow the rules and now answer the question: "What one piece of advice you would give to someone?"

You need to have a solid business model and plan!

Our model and plan start with vision and solution(s) to a big problem, need, or want.

Next, you need a clearly articulated message of exactly what is your vision; how you can achieve that vision; and how you can solve a big problem, need, or want.

You cannot build your business machine until you have the vision and the message!

Your next step is putting the vision, message, and plan in motion through a solid business model and plan:

- Never stop letting the world know what your vision is and how you are going to solve their problem, need, or want.

- Consistently execute consistency through marketing, closing, and delivery of your product and or service that goes above and beyond the client's expectation.
- Continuously, at all points, analyze and optimize the vision, plan, and process, making necessary adjustments as needed.
- Innovate, innovate, and innovate because when you stop, there lies the next best thing ready to take your position and replace you in an instant.
- Technological advancement must always be at the forefront of your world never hindering human creativity but rather enhancing and allowing the creative juices to flow and explode.
- Never ever forget about your team, because you are who you are because of your team.
- Always make sure you are properly capitalized at all times; without capital you are finished before you start.
- Always make sure you know your ROI (return on investment) objectives and strive to exceed those goals.
- Always seek mentorship and coaching from experts and successful people.

This is about humanity, the earth, and our belief system—nothing more and nothing less.

Dream it, build it, innovate it, and deliver it above expectations, and you too shall be successful on what will be one of the most rewarding journeys on which you will ever embark!

Create your business model and plan today.

About Eric

Eric Holtz leads the Core & Start Base Team and is the founder of BusinessProfit2.2.

Eric is an entrepreneur of over thirty years, owning businesses in diverse industries. He has been involved with distribution, manufacturing, and service industries as well as nonprofit groups.

Eric's mission in starting BusinessProfit2.2 is to share his knowledge with other businesses and organizations, giving them a huge organizational advantage and saving years of trial and error. Going through good times and bad, several economic downturns, and the 2008 national recession has forged his viewpoints on how businesses should be setup and structured to remain profitable.

Eric sees things through an entrepreneurial perspective and understands first-hand what a business owner and leader goes through on a daily basis.

About Eric's Company
BusinessProfit2.2
Consulting
www.BusinessProfitConsulting.com

Create Your Soul-Based Business Plan

D. KAY HUTCHINSON

Founder • Owner

How I Got My Start

Imagine a feeling of liberation and the capacity to expand in many different directions creatively. Imagine a life where one does not have others hampering that expression in business and the thrilling challenge of making a living by working for yourself. Yes, it's exciting and filled with autonomy but also filled with great responsibility and the necessity for laser focus and deep insights about how to understand and produce multiple revenue streams.

I have worked as an entrepreneur in many capacities since I was 27 years old. What prompted me to start the latest endeavor 17 years ago, Aiki Healing, a holistic practice of medicine and school, was realizing that many people are simply not functioning at their optimal level on a brain, body, emotional, and spiritual level. This impacts our leadership skills as business owners and what we create and put into the world. However, most people are too busy to make major health changes until a catastrophic illness absolutely forces them to slow down and build better balance into their lifestyles.

My intention with Aiki Healing was to design a system of strategies that could be implemented by very busy people, as they move through their days, to gently transform habits and patterns that play a role in not being able to access their true and deep selves. My own journey with recovering my health, after years of suffering with fibromyalgia while running a high-tech company in Silicon Valley, also played a role in the deep understanding of my clients' schedules and the stress loads in terms of developing the customized solutions that I provide to them.

My Advice to Aspiring Business Owners and Entrepreneurs
It is so important to choose a direction in business that reflects your genuine passions and to invest the time to develop what I call a soul-based business plan, a business plan that not only covers the traditional areas of marketing, branding, analysis of products and services compared to competitors, analysis of costs expenditures and projecttions of revenue for services and products, etcetera but one that also maps the strategy for leadership self-growth and self-care as you move through the different stages of developing your business.

This self-growth part of the plan includes an analysis of the tools that are necessary to keep you and other leadership staff at optimal performance including life coaching/mentoring, health insurance, traditional western medical appointments, holistic care, revival time activities such as vacations (and how to create blended work/revival experiences so that you can write-off some of your travel and self-care expenses), nutrition (how to fuel your body through your busy days), and how to build an inner circle of support for you as a growing person (not just a business networking group).

This self-growth and self-care plan may also influence you to develop, within your traditional part of the business plan, budgets for helping other staff to care-take themselves well such as incorporating three-day weekends, something corporations such as Microsoft are implementing. Microsoft discovered that when employees have longer down time, their productivity at work improved by forty percent.

Entrepreneurs who take as much time to plan their personal growth plans as they do their traditional business plans have longevity in their business cycles and create an energy that attracts customers, staff, and business partners because they shine with the energy of their true selves, which are being nourished through the process of mindfully building their businesses. To summarize, we need to go beyond traditional business plans to encompass a leadership self-care plan as entrepreneurs, so we have the mental sharpness, emotional stability, abundant physical health, and spiritual drive to build our businesses with balance.

About Kay

What do education, high tech, and healing arts have in common? Kay Hutchinson.

I started my career as a triple-certified educator working in a public school and designing educational curricula for students with special needs and for students in mainstreamed classroom settings. After a back injury on the job, I channeled my passion for education and the desire to help others into a freelance career, writing for *Tech & Learning* magazine and as a contract writer for an Austin-based publisher's resource house that served publishing giants such as Prentice Hall, Silver Burdett Gin, and Holt. I loved being a part of teams, developing innovative teacher guides and textbooks that emphasized holistic methods of learning where activities encouraged students to grow personally as well as academically.

Later, I built a successful career in Silicon Valley working as a contract usability and website content developer for Lyris Technologies and other clients. I also ghost wrote white papers and trade articles for top executives in Silicon Valley.

In all of these capacities, I saw my job as helping people use education and technology to create meaningful transformations in people's lives. I later founded InSync Web with the core mission of using websites to create transformations. InSync Web focused on developing organic websites in a process that involved deep interviews with clients to understand their business missions in ways that helped our clients connect even more deeply with their passions and to communicate their passions and solutions via the web in a soul-based way.

Although I was riding the wave of the dot-com boom era, I made sure to cultivate brick-and-mortar clients—mostly healers involved with the field of Chinese medicine. While working with them, they noticed the natural affinity that I had for understanding the concepts from that field; they encouraged me to go back to school. Thus, I simultaneously enrolled in the integral counseling program at California Institute of Integral Studies (CIIS) in San Francisco, a graduate school of transpersonal psychology (a nontraditional psychotherapy program that looks at how we develop not only emotionally but also spiritually), and the Longevity Institute (a three-year training program for medical qi gong, the most ancient form of Chinese medicine that pre-dates acupuncture and that uses energy healing methods, herbs, and nutrition to help people grow holistic-ally).

I was mentored by Dr. Arnold Tayam who not only founded the school but was also the head qi gong instructor who developed several programs for patients and training doctors at Stanford Integrative Medicine Department. Later, I put my full emphasis on training with Chinese medicine and also expanded to study at the Acupressure Institute in Berkeley, studying with Michael Gach, world famous for his best-selling books on acupressure.

In 2003, I began working as an acupressurist in San Jose, California, and then later moved to the Austin, Texas area in 2005 to be near my aging parents. My focus in those days was geriatric care and cancer recovery, but over the years. I expanded the work to include a myriad of health issues. As I worked with clients to help them transform their lifestyles in a natural way that dove-tailed with their busy lives, many of them went on to create their own businesses, often in the health care or service industries, but they were interested in learning more about the methods I use in my practice.

These clients encouraged me to create the Aiki Healing certification program, the only school of medical qi gong that is comprehensive (three years) and that taught entirely through private mentoring. Just as I had developed custom healing protocols that my clients could integrate into their busy lives, I also developed a training program curriculum that is customized to individual students so that they can learn deeply, optimally, and in a very personalized way. It is the only program of Chinese medicine in Texas that certifies professionals in modules so that students can begin working in the field to gain real world experience as they continue to learn. Thus, Aiki Healing graduates are highly trained with practical experience before they finish their final hours.

Aiki Healing training program also encourages students who live outside of Texas to learn through technologies such as Zoom. The use of video technology also allows Aiki Healing to provide students with training materials that allow them to review hands-on training sessions in the comfort of their own homes and in a way that fits their schedules.

Aiki Healing also works with other organizations in terms of job placement and securing contracts for graduates to help build their practices and expand possibilities for greater healing for all people with programs that include flex-fees and sliding scales as well as pro bono strands.

About Kay's Company

Aiki Healing

Aiki Healing specializes in customized holistic healing solutions that integrate with clients' busy lives and provides a three-year professional certification program in the ancient art of medical qi gong (the precursor to acupuncture) that is taught entirely through private mentoring that is customized to students' interests and schedules. We transform stuck lives into blooming potential and teach others how to be healing forces of light in the world.

www.aikihealing.com

Plan to Scale from the Very Beginning

LA'VISTA JONES, CLBC

Systems & Self-Care Consultant • Speaker • Author • Coach

How I Got My Start

I started my company because my soul ached watching ambitious, passionate, and talented visionaries burn themselves out trying to do everything all on their own.

Visionaries amaze me with their creativity to introduce unique ideas into the marketplace. They possess an endless source of care to nurture, grow, and develop those ideas. Moreover, visionaries yield the business acumen to map out strategies to guide the trajectory of those ideas. In addition, they reflect the flexible tenacity needed to navigate and endure the valleys, hurdles, and setbacks encountered along the entrepreneurial journey.

However, visionaries sometimes have the tendency to dismiss the importance of surrounding themselves with the support and resources they need—often resulting in pushing their self-care to the bottom of their to-do lists.

These are the overwhelmed, flirting-with-burnout type of visionaries with whom I love working.

Part of my magic is being naturally wired to see the missing pieces, the gaps, and the ways to improve upon a process.

Prior to launching my business, I considered this to be an off-putting trait of mine. When someone would share a business idea with me, my internal dialogue consisted of notes about what needed to be changed or fixed. It wasn't until my early twenties that I began to realize that this trait of mine was actually a valuable skill set—one that would create opportunities for me to serve and support other entrepreneurs, corporate partners, non-profits, and ministries.

I founded my company, 31 Marketplace in 2005, after having a conversation with my friend, Mike.

We met up to talk through opportunities within his graphic design business. During our conversation, he suddenly looked at me and said, matter-of-fact-like, "You know, you should be doing this as a business."

Baffled by his statement, I remember responding, "No, people don't really need this type of support."

Determined to prove his point, Mike started bringing up examples of how I'd already helped our mutual friends get their lives together by streamlining their businesses and prioritizing time for themselves.

At the moment, I dismissed Mike's idea of launching a business. But later that same evening, I kept finding myself replaying our conversation in my head over and over again.

Armed with inspired curiosity, I started asking my friends, who also happened to be business owners, for their feedback about the professional service I was interested in providing. And unanimously. one after another, they each admitted that they'd wished they had known a long time ago that I could have helped them in this way.

And that was all it took.

After filing the necessary paperwork, I immediately quit my corporate gig and set out to bring 31 Marketplace to visionaries worldwide.

My Advice to Aspiring Business Owners and Entrepreneurs

If you're thinking of starting a business, be mindful of how you want to scale it from the beginning, and build out your processes every step of the way.

In the early stages of a business, the owner usually wears all of the hats: marketing, sales, operations, fulfillment, etcetera. In the beginning phase, it can be manageable—easy even—to do everything alone. So much so that a mindset of "get-it-done-myself" without support or outsourcing can set in.

But that couldn't be further from the truth.

Vision is not a solo mission.

Other people, resources, and assistance are all needed to bring a vision to fruition. Invest the time and money into your business to document your processes, best practices, and internal policies from day one. This not only creates operational assets within your business, but it will increase the efficiency and effectiveness of your future team.

And don't worry if you're not an operational guru, your internal documentation isn't required to be complex; it just needs to be done.

About La'Vista

La'Vista Jones, CLBC helps her clients bring order to the chaos of life and business. She believes the price of success doesn't have to include burnout and broken promises to yourself. By discovering a better way to run your business, you can get back to making yourself and what you love a priority.

As an author, speaker, and community builder, La'Vista is leading a movement of visionaries who want more from life than frazzled days and sleepless nights. Her unique magic is helping business owners get shit done without burning themselves out. Her work allows you to add time back to your day by streamlining processes, identifying operational gaps, and outsourcing.

An Ohio native, La'Vista currently resides in Arizona with her husband; their son, 'The Cub;' and fur baby, Bull Dozer.

About La'Vista's Company

31 Marketplace

Systems and Self-Care Consultancy

www.thirtyonemarketplace.com

Learn What You Can While On Someone Else's Payroll

SHAWNTÉ JONES
Coach • Published Author • Public Speaker

How I Got My Start

Your environment and that to which you are exposed when you are growing up shape how you interact in life when you become an adult. Because I grew up in a low-income, rural environment with blue collar, working parents, my career outlook was limited to what I saw in my family, at school, and what I read about in my favorite mystery novels. Not only was my career outlook limited but so was the network of positive influences to help me figure out how to accomplish the desires of achieving more than a high school diploma. What was instilled in me was to work hard, and what I enjoyed was learning. That combination was helpful to me as a young adult.

Early on, what I had going for me was my initiative, drive, and a personality that my professors liked. My first break into the corporate environment was because of one of my professors. I recall her telling me that I wasn't like the other girls. What I did not realize at the time was that she was observing me to determine whether I was worthy of her taking the risk of offering me an opportunity to co-op at a Fortune 500 company. What I also did not realize at the time, but over time in reflection it came to me, was that what I felt I was missing in how I grew up was also missing in some of my college classmates and co-workers—despite their upbringing, culture or socio-economic status. Upon entry and spending a career in human resources, I realized that even educated people from diverse backgrounds still struggled with having an expanded career outlook and in building a network of positive influencers. As a person who had to figure out things on my own, I learned a lot through observation and first-hand experience of what works and what does not work.

In getting the co-op opportunity, I learned that people are always watching, assessing, and formulating opinions about me even if I do not see or know they are doing it. I do not know whether "those other girls" ever received feedback about what caused them to be looked over for an opportunity that they likely did not know existed, but that situation and others like it caused me to become interested in coaching others about their personal and professional development.

Once I became a full-time employee, I began by going back to my former college to speak to co-op students, then I started giving advice and recommendations to co-workers during conversations about their personal lives or careers. Initially, I did not put a label on what I was doing because I was looking to help people who were willing to listen and better position and prepare themselves for better opportunities. I eventually began hosting workshops focusing on career management and personal accountability. Once my career in human resources further developed, I became more aware of my unique position and potential impact in assisting others in their personal and professional development. I launched my business because I know there are individuals out there who need help getting from one point in their career to the next point.

Be Bold Enterprises is dedicated to personal and professional development. I focus on serving early to mid-level career professionals in positioning themselves to gain exposure that will elevate their careers to the next level. Years working in human resources with managers at multiple levels within the organization gave me insight on what they look for in employees as well as what turns them off. Gaining a certificate in personal development coaching helped me establish how to work with my clients, but my best training ground was gained from my employment experience from working in human resources.

My Advice to Aspiring Business Owners and Entrepreneurs
Advice that I would give to someone wanting to become an entrepreneur is this: While you are employed, learn what you can on someone else's payroll until you have what you need to step out on your own. This means to take advantage of whom and that to which you are already exposed in your role, being mindful of not violating intellectual property, confidentiality agreements, code of conduct guidelines or plagiarism. Here are some tips to leverage your learnings to the benefit of your future entrepreneurship.

Ask questions that are relevant to your current employment but are also transferable to your potential business. For example, if you work in supply chain or procurement, you can ask questions to learn more about sourcing and the customer relationship management (CRM) system to apply to your current role, but the learnings you gain can be leveraged in your business. You can also ask questions that will increase your business acumen. This is beneficial to you because you are learning more about how business works, and you are gaining a deeper understanding about business lingo. The more you learn about business allows you to make more informed decisions relating to your responsibilities at work and will also benefit you personally, especially if you do not have a business degree.

Be willing to volunteer on projects at work. When you work on project teams, you are expanding your knowledge and increasing your problem-solving skills. Project management, whether you lead the project or not, gives you valuable experience. Being on a project team, you will learn about lean tools to track project status, implementation processes, negotiation skills, deadline management, budgeting, conflict resolution, and other key skills required to make a project successful that will serve you well as a leader of your own company.

Create a network of future potential clients. No poaching! Build your client network honestly. Learn who in your organization may have a need for what you plan to offer in your company. Don't be deceptive. Let them know that you have an interest in that specific area, ask their opinions, and conduct informal questionnaires. If they are your target market, then analyze them by being observant, and test your ideas by offering suggestions and recommendations. Keep in mind that potential clients may also be family, friends, or past co-workers of your current co-workers. You can explore who is in their network by building rapport with them. I secured several career development clients because of organically built relationships with co-workers. If people like you, they will speak about you to others in their network.

As previously mentioned, people watch you, make assessments about you, and formulate opinions of you without you knowing. If you are delivering on your commitments for your employer, people will expect that when you transition to becoming an entrepreneur. Let your output for your employer showcase to potential clients or client connectors what you are capable of achieving. You don't know who a lead to clients can be, so show your best self each opportunity you can.

About Shawnté

Shawnté Jones is the owner of Be Bold Enterprises, LLC and focuses on coaching early to mid-level professionals to get noticed in the workplace and move to the next level in their careers.

Shawnté has over fifteen years of experience working for large chemical manufacturing companies in human resources. She holds a Bachelor of Arts degree in communication and a Master of Science degree in human resource development. Shawnté also has a certificate in personal development coaching. She coached students in public speaking as an adjunct instructor for several semesters at the college level. She is now also a member of the John Maxwell Team.

Shawnté's first book, *I Have Talents, And I am Not Afraid to Use Them* is the ideal read for those who want to overcome the fears that are holding them back from reaching the level of success they desire. Recently, she collaborated in writing *On Purpose: Practical Strategies to Live Your Best Life*, which is a compilation of strategies that will help readers get their lives on the right track.

About Shawnté's Company
Be Bold Enterprises, LLC
Personal and Professional Development
www.thebeboldenterprises.com

Always Believe in Your Vision

RUCHI G. KALRA
Coach • Author • Storyteller

How I Got My Start

I started my business to help businesses tell their stories. Most small business owners struggle with their passion, vision, and execution, and through it all, their stories get lost. By definition, a small business owner has to wear multiple hats, but sometimes in that process, they lose the WHY they started their businesses in the first place.

Many small business owners are so busy working on their business that sometimes it's hard for them to step back and look at the big picture. I like to help businesses get back to what they love and their reasons for starting their businesses, and I sit down with them and take them back to the beginning with a set of thought-provoking questions. Through this vision session, I am not only able to understand their passion for pursuing their businesses or their dream projects in the first place but where their businesses are currently.

Through our sessions, they are better able to understand that they do not have to have a huge marketing budget to make an impact. I show them ways on how to better understand their networks within their local communities to build meaningful relationships and valued connections that, in turn, promote business growth. We work together to make their messages authentic and believable so their true vision of the business can shine through. I show them that authenticity attracts and retains real and loyal customers. People may not always love their content or even their products, but they will fall in love with their realness and their courage to be vulnerable and to put themselves out there; and this will fuel their passion for support for the business.

I help re-build their belief and inspire and encourage them to take action to get back to their "WHY" through authenticity of themselves and their business.

My Advice to Aspiring Business Owners and Entrepreneurs

Always believe in your vision, and never let anyone tell you that you can't do something. But, also never be scared to know when it's time to say "goodbye" to that vision if it comes down to that. I have had a few businesses that I have worked hard at making succeed, but for the ones that didn't, I never looked at them as failures. We and only we can set our own definition of failure and success. I learned so much from each and every one of them through the process—from not only the relationships that I built but also the mistakes that I made. Every single experience taught me something to take forward to my next venture.

Ruchi doesn't believe in the thirty-second elevator pitches as she believes that so much gets lost in those memorized pitches. There is so much more depth to us than that, and it's time to unshackle ourselves from those. So, please do read my bio to get a snippet of my story.

About Ruchi

She was born in India, moved to Africa when she was nine, and has lived in the U.S since she moved there for college at fifteen. Yes, she started college at fifteen, but that's a whole other story. She has always been a people person and spends a lot of time on relationship-building and employs the same philosophies in her marketing approaches. She has a Bachelor of Science in math and computer science and an MBA in marketing. She is married to her childhood sweetheart and has two kids—a rising college freshman and a rising senior, both at Emory University in Atlanta. But her favorite of all is her fur baby they rescued two years ago.

Over the years, she has worked in various roles in revenue accounting/sales planning and analysis to marketing for an orthodontist. Ruchi has her own coaching firm, Dancing Raindrops Inc., to help small businesses tell their stories so they can let their and their businesses' true messages shine through authentically.

About Ruchi's Company

Dancing Raindrops Inc.
Business Coaching
dancingraindropsinc.com

Clarify Your Intention for Your Business

VERED KOGAN

Executive Coach • Professional Speaker • Change Management Expert

How I Got My Start

I initially started my coaching business because I wanted to do something meaningful that would also allow me to have the flexibility I needed as a mom. You see, I took a break from my corporate career a few years earlier to raise my three daughters, and I was eager to get back to the "work world" when my youngest entered kindergarten.

When I considered what I wanted to do in the next chapter of my career, I remembered the life-changing experience I had with a coach after I was laid-off from a job due to a large corporate acquisition. It was a very difficult time in my life. I experienced many emotions like frustration, sadness, and fear. I started doubting my abilities, and my self-confidence took a deep dive. Thankfully, I was given the opportunity by my employer to work with a career coach for six months. Michael, my coach, helped me shift my focus away from the present reality and toward future possibilities. He helped me reconnect with my inner power and believe in myself again. I didn't know it back then, but this experience altered the course of my life in a profound way. I learned that I truly get to create my own reality through my choice of focus. And it inspired me to become a professional coach so I could help others experience a similar transformation and create the life of their dreams. Like many of you, I received this great gift on the other side of a painful life experience.

Once I made the decision to launch a coaching business, everything changed. Although I did not yet know how to build a business or what type of coach I wanted to be, I felt energized because I knew in my heart that I will get to help people. I started coming up with all kinds of ideas regarding next steps. For example, I remember meeting a coach who volunteered with me at a local women's resource center, and I got the impulse to reach out and ask what type of coach training she received. Within an hour, I reached out to the school and signed up for a year-long program. I did not yet know where it would all lead, but I was fully committed to my vision. It felt congruent, and I trusted my intuition.

One conversation led to another, one action led to another, and one coaching client led to another. Over time, I understood more clearly what I loved and that of which I needed to let go. As my income grew, I started hiring people to help me with things like developing website and bookkeeping so I could focus on the things that bring me more meaning and fulfillment.

Nowadays, I continue to focus on the same three things every day that assure my company's success: doing my best to help my clients, improving my skills, and being present with the people in my life. Staying focused on these three things help me to get unstuck when I'm not sure of the next right step and stay aligned with the deeper purpose of my business.

My Advice to Aspiring Business Owners and Entrepreneurs

The one piece of advice I would give to someone who wants to start a business is to clarify your intention for the business. You must connect with the deeper purpose for your business and how you want to help others.

You see, starting a business is, in many ways, like walking around a house at night, bumping into walls and furniture and feeling lost and uncertain. Specifying a simple, clear and emotionally meaningful intention is like having a flashlight. You can turn it on at any time to feel grounded, get focused, and see your next right step.

Many entrepreneurs and business owners do not take the time to clarify or continuously practice their "guiding purpose." They tend to respond to unexpected or stressful situations in a very reactive way, which gets projected onto others and limits their ability to inspire confidence or to build trust. I believe that being intentional is a vital mindset for effective leadership and a successful business. It's about making decisions and taking actions in alignment with your values and your organization's purpose.

The guiding purpose for my business is to, "Inspire and empower people to achieve their full potential in life and business." Any time I make a decision regarding whether to accept a coaching client, agree to a speaking engagement, attend a training, write a blog, or contribute to a book like this, I ask myself whether the decision is aligned with my intention. If the answer is "yes," then I will move towards that opportunity. If the answer is "no," then I will turn it down, even when there are aspects of the opportunity that seem attractive. Although being intentional does not guarantee that I will always make the right decision, it does allow me to feel congruent about my choices so that I step out of my comfort zone and take more risks.

Ask yourself "What is important to me in the context of my business?" Then, prioritize the list and write a clear, simple, and positive "guiding purpose" statement. This powerful intention can serve as your "flashlight" any time you get lost and want to feel more congruent regarding the next right step in your business.

About Vered

Vered Kogan is an executive coach, speaker, and author with a unique ability for helping people release the mental and emotional obstacles that prevent them from achieving their full potential in life and business. As a leading behavioral and mindset expert, her personal vision is to help millions of people adapt more effectively to change by leveraging the power of their subconscious mind.

Vered began her career as a civil engineer, graduating from the University of Toronto. After working in structural testing at an aerospace manufacturer, she went on to earn an MBA from the Schulich School of Business, specializing in strategic management. Vered then joined PricewaterhouseCoopers as a management consultant, helping business executives prepare their organizations for change. After moving to the U.S. from Canada, Vered went on to receive a Certificate in Human Resource Management from the University of Dallas Graduate School of Management.

Vered is accredited by the International Coach Federation (ICF) and holds numerous other professional coaching credentials. As a Trainer of Neuro-Linguistic Programming (NLP), Time Line Therapy®, and Hypnosis, she is an expert on shifting subconscious patterns. Vered is also certified in other leading mind technologies such as Rapid Transformational Therapy®, Psych-K®, HeartMath®, and Yoga Nidra.

Vered has coached hundreds of executives and entrepreneurs in her coaching practice, Vered Kogan Coaching. She offers a variety of coaching programs, live workshops, and keynotes on topics such as mindset, resilience, and change management to help individuals thrive in our increasingly complex world.

Vered has volunteered at the Fresh Start Women's Foundation since 2005 to support women through personal and career transitions. She currently lives in Arizona with her husband, Paul, and their three daughters.

About Vered's Company

Vered Kogan Coaching, LLC

Personal and Professional Development

www.veredkogan.com

Learn as Much as You Can

CHRISTINA KUMAR
Award-Winning Entrepreneur

How I Got My Start

As a child, I started selling things to my neighbors and was creating blueprints for products and retail business by the time I was twelve. As a preteen, I would practice marketing and selling because I loved it so much. It was a thrill. I always had an interest in becoming an entrepreneur, and I have a strong internal drive towards it to this day. I love the freedom it brings, and being able to have businesses in many fields is awesome because it helps me to get creative with my work. I was very creative when I was younger and loved to make things as well, so it is important that I am still able to be creative today.

I naturally gravitate towards anything entrepreneurial—books, people, magazines, ideas, places—you name it! I love watching ideas grow; it's exciting. I knew I was going to be a business owner and would daydream about it. Now it's popular to be an entrepreneur, and I have seen the resources growing tremendously for entrepreneurs in the last several years. Being born in California, I think, has

187

had a positive impact on me getting into entrepreneurship early. I tend to be optimistic even in the most difficult circumstances and will see the positive in most situations. Also being close to the Silicon Valley helps too; it's mind-blowing how many talented entrepreneurs are located there. I am also around business owners and entrepreneurs often, and the energy is catchy.

Starting my businesses required me to know legal aspects, marketing, and website development, which I learned prior to starting. I could have hired a team for this, but I wanted to have more control and confidence over these aspects; so I decided to do these myself. I also wanted to know more because I can then be more hands-on and not have to rely so much on other people to run my businesses. I think being able to make my own decisions is a big factor of why I am an entrepreneur today. I was always someone who acted on things before consulting with anyone because I didn't want to get talked out of my decisions. I think that as a leader, you do have to go with your own gut feelings at times.

My Advice to Aspiring Business Owners and Entrepreneurs

Learn as much as you can. You can save so much time and stress doing this early. It is important to know the good and the bad in business because if you only expect the flowers and sunshine, then how are you going to get through the storms when you are not prepared? Also, definitely get an advisor to help guide you so you don't feel isolated. They can also help you to avoid potential issues. Keep learning new skills because businesses require so many skills, and it's good to be on top of that which can grow your business.

Act fast when there's an issue because it can cost you more in the end. I was given advice by a well-known entrepreneur who had said to get a good lawyer, a good accountant, and a good insurance person; I definitely recommend this advice. When you grow, you need to keep your business safe. I also recommend treating everyone with respect because in the future, they can be your best advocates as well as customers. Also, try new things! Customers want something new; that is why the traditional approach is being replaced. Today, we have next day shipping, twenty-four-hour online shopping, live customer service; these services have become an expectation. It is important to get as close to expectations as possible to better serve our customers because the happier customers are, the more they will recommend your business to other people and will be more likely to leave good reviews, which will, in return, bring in new customers.

About Christina

Christina Kumar is an award-winning entrepreneur and journalist. She has won a Google for Entrepreneurs powered competition, which kick-started her business journey, and since then, she has opened a public relations agency and fashion store. She has worked with both Emmy-award winning talent as well as Olympic athletes in obtaining public relations for their brands. She is passionate about helping fellow entrepreneurs grow and frequently advises them on ways to expand.

About Christina's Company

Christina Kumar PR
Public Relations
www.christinakumar.com

Start with a Side Hustle

MONIKA LABBÉ
Professional Photographer

How I Got My Start

I started my business as a side hustle while working for Corporate America in human resources. At that time, I did not think about having my business be my sole source of income. Because it was a side hustle, I could be choosy about the projects that I wanted to take on; it gave me lots of creative freedom. My work has evolved from film to digital, from part-time to full-time, and from only photographing weddings to portraiture. It has allowed me to explore different genres and to decide what it was that truly made my heart bounce in photography. In the beginning, it was a lot of trial and error, and in a lot of different ways, being a woman photographer was being a pioneer as twenty years ago, photography was largely a male dominated field of expertise. The Internet, at that time, was not what it is today, and social media was nonexistent. Everything was built upon organic reach and excellent customer service.

Although no one in my immediate family had his/her own business, having an entrepreneurial spirit was something that was handed down to me from my grandparents. They taught me the value of persistence and perseverance and most of all, resilience. In my opinion, being entrepreneurial is an essential ingredient to success in business.

My Advice to Aspiring Business Owners and Entrepreneurs

If you are wanting to have a full-time business, start it as a side hustle and see how it's going first. If you are your sole source of support, then make sure you have ample savings to float you during peaks and valleys. If you have a partner to financially support you during this time, then make sure you have a game plan not just for the first year but for the years going forward. Set-up systems, and try to automate as much as possible so you are not spending every moment on your business. Always have an out strategy just in case you need one.

Decide before you begin what you need and what would make you quit and/or sell the business. Find mentors that are already successful in the business whom you would like to launch and hire them to coach you on what you need to position yourself for success. Also, network with people, and surround yourself with positive people who are successful in other businesses. The people who you surround yourself with every day have a great impact on you and your emotional state. Create a vision board of the life you want to lead with your business, then focus on making it happen!

About Monika

When I was a child, I wanted to be a doctor. I loved taking the heads off my dolls to see what was inside them. I had a huge imagination and lots of curiosity. My family was largely in the medical field, so I was around a lot of service-minded professionals. I was always drawing and painting most of my life. At age ten, I received my first camera from my father. This quickly became my favorite thing to do, and I took photos of everything and everyone. The only thing that limited me was the twenty-four exposures on the roll, and that it took money to develop and buy film.

In high school, I was a member of the National Art Honor Society. My artwork was sent on a nationwide tour for students with the most artistic promise. In college, I majored in advertising, design, and illustration and was the photo editor for the school newspaper. I then went on to get an additional degree in human behavior. I had briefly considered being a clinical psychologist, but soon after graduation, I got a job in human resources and decided to stick with it. But when the housing market crashed and companies started laying off, I suddenly found myself at a crossroad. I contemplated looking for work, but as more and more companies were downsizing, I thought this was a good time as any to go for it. It was never my intention to try to grow a business in the worst economy ever. With social media starting to get popular, it was the perfect time to start sharing photos with my friends and family, and suddenly my photography was gaining momentum. It seemed everyone needed a new LinkedIn photo and or had an event coming up, and soon I was busier than ever.

About Monika's Company
Creative M Portraits
Photography
www.creativeMportraits.com

Find Quality Sources, People, and Organizations

DR. ANA LARA
Naturopathic Medical Doctor • Healer • Entrepreneur

How I Got My Start

My journey is an accumulation of life events that led me to open my own business. Growing up in a low socioeconomic region and being a first-generation American, as a young girl, I witnessed many disparities and experienced much adversities in my life. Nevertheless, I continued to persist and move forward to every goal I set myself to accomplish. At the young age of twenty-seven, I found myself ill and extremely exhausted. As I worked hard to climb the imaginary "ladder of success," it was taking a toll on me. I worked and went to school full-time and was active in several nonprofit organizations in my community. As a Mexican American, I was taking notice of the challenges involved with a woman trying to move up in management in Corporate America. It had very little to do with skillset, experience, or education; they didn't like people who were outspoken or direct or who challenged the system or questioned things. I always had a desire to be a business owner, but at this point, I was too sick to even consider the move.

Though I was educated and determined to find solutions to my health, doctors were never helpful to me. They didn't listen to my needs. I was constantly told "Your labs look fine. There is nothing else we can do." I went from doctor to doctor until I decided to take ownership of my health and made changes. Over time, I would start the healing—all through natural means—that, for many years, I had put off. I was healing through the emotional pain that I held in for so many years. I was healing through the mental anguish from not speaking my truth. I was healing spiritually to feel free from all burdens. Reconnecting to my Higher Power was liberating. Only then was I able to find healing in my physical body. It was after all this happened that I awakened to my calling. I went on to become a naturopathic medical doctor because I knew it would allow me the best of both worlds: conventional medicine and natural medicine. From the moment I made my decision to move in this direction, I knew in my heart I would not work for someone else. I would not give my power and control to someone else on how I saw myself working to help people heal.

I started my business to provide a place for people who were yearning to find healing, to find solutions, and get their life back. I want to give people the opportunity to experience what I have experienced in rejuvenating my physical, mental, emotional, and spiritual bodies. "Why?" you ask. It's because you don't know what you are missing out in life until you remove the obstacles and can then clearly see for yourself and experience life through a different lens. I know that for myself, when the dark grey cloud was lifted and I began to experience life fully, I made connections that I couldn't before. These connections led me to making different decisions for myself and my family. It made me a happy, fulfilled person. I want to help create a world of people who are happy, fulfilled, and who can spread their own gifts to the world. The world is a much better place when people are happy, compassionate, and fully present. My business is to help others blossom into this spark of JOY. I get to witness my clients blossom and spread their wings. I literally get chills, and my eyes fill with tears to see the metamorphosis of them into the highest version of themselves.

My Advice to Aspiring Business Owners and Entrepreneurs

My advice to someone who wants to start a business is to start by finding quality sources, and people, or organizations that can help you. If you don't have the business background, skills, or entrepreneurial mindset, go out and find it. Learn to ask for help. There are so many resources that offer help; don't think you have to do it all alone. Find out what you need to do to start off on the right foot. Yet, don't wait for things to be perfect to start. Follow the 80/20 rule: if you are 80% ready, then that is good enough to start; for the rest, you will build on it. You will figure out a lot as you go through building your business. Create your business plan, and make it a living entity; continue to work on it, and regularly turn to it to ensure you are living up to your mission, vision, and goals.

Hire a good attorney, a certified public accountant (CPA), and a bookkeeper! They are worth the investment. Get a good understanding of all areas of your business, and figure out who you need to hire. The important areas of business to be familiar with are law, insurance, bookkeeping, accounting, financial, marketing/advertising, and then all the areas specific to your industry.

It's important to define what is your "why". What do you love to do that you could do all day? What brings you purpose? What are you passionate and excited about? Understand your target market or ideal client so you can be more precise in your marketing efforts. Once you define the need of your target market, you can be genuine in your marketing.

If you are starting a partnership, take the time to really get to know each other, and ask yourself the tough questions. While I don't like to bring this up, I know that someone out there could benefit from my experience. I started out as a partnership; we made the time to create a partnership agreement, and we met with an attorney to finalize and legitimize the operating agreement. We discussed all the pros and cons, and the "what ifs." Into our first year, I didn't foresee how this partnership would work out; we were going in different directions. Going through a business separation is like a divorce. Here is what I learned and things you should ask yourself and your partner.

1. Who was the first to mention working together? If the other person approached you first, would you have also approached him/her about entering into business if he/she had not brought up the idea? In other words, did you pick him/her or did he/she pick you? If you wouldn't have initially picked that person as a business partner, then slow down. Take the time to fully assess. You should both be

choosing each other and be driven only on emotion to make this decision. It's a business marriage.

2. What do you each bring as qualities, experiences, or talents to starting a business? If you are "unequally yoked," you will have challenges later on. One partner may feel he/she is doing most of the work; and that is overwhelming over time.

3. What kind of family planning do you need to take into consideration so as to cause minimal disruption to the business? While family planning affects both men and women, let's be honest; most of the time, a woman carries most of the burden. It's just the way it is. As a woman, we are the ones who get pregnant; deliver a baby, nurse; and deal with physical, mental and emotional shifts during and after pregnancy, etcetera. It's normal. Being a mother myself, and a doctor, I know what these changes do to your brain. There is such a thing called pregnancy brain or postpartum brain. However, when you are building a business, it's going to affect your mental focus and physical energy. We live in a culture where we think we can do it all. We can, but at what price? There is always a price we pay. Either the business suffers, or you suffer with your health or both. Have the conversation on family planning goals, and come to a mutual agreement of timing of these life events. The first five years of starting a business is hard work but especially in the first two years while you establish some routines and get an idea of where your business is in this time period. Being pregnant in the first year of a business is a huge no! This means the partner will have to be on maternity leave for a period of time. Will you be okay with that time off or having limitations on working full-time on the business?

4. How will you handle disputes? Be realistic. Will you assign a mediator if you cannot come to a decision on disputes?

5. How will you handle enforcing the business operating agreement and partnership responsibilities?

6. What legal representation do you need? I can't emphasize this enough: Hire an attorney! Complete your operating agreement/partnership agreement, have an attorney draft it for you, review it together, and sign it.

About Ana

Dr. Ana Lara is a Phoenix, Arizona native, a community that she has served over her lifetime. Dr. Lara is a licensed naturopathic physician in the state of Arizona. Dr. Lara graduated with honors from the University of Phoenix with a Bachelor of Science in Business/Finance and an MBA. Due to her journey with her own health, she became interested in nutrition and holistic health. She reversed type II diabetes and Hashimoto's Thyroiditis (an autoimmune thyroid condition) on her own using diet, botanical medicine, and other natural therapies. After regaining her health, she attended and earned her doctorate in naturopathic medicine from Southwest College of Naturopathic Medicine and Health Sciences in Tempe, Arizona.

Prior to becoming a naturopathic medical doctor, Dr. Lara worked in various businesses in law, finance, banking, financial planning, real estate, and academia. This helped her with founding her own company later on.

She is the founder and owner of Raíces Naturopathic Medical Center, PLLC in Phoenix, Arizona. Dr. Lara takes an interest in treating the whole person, not just treating symptoms. She uses the most effective natural treatments in conjunction with the latest medical research. At Raíces, it's a priority to create a healing and calming atmosphere where there are no wait times, and the time is invested to listening to the patient and providing education or therapies. People are heard, validated, and helped in deep, profound ways.

Her practice focus includes family medicine, pediatrics, women's health, clinical nutrition, metabolic disorders, pain management, mental/emotional conditions, endocrine disorders, neurological disorders, chronic, and autoimmune diseases including chronic pain. She is an expert in preventing and treating type II diabetes, thyroid disorders, and autoimmune conditions.

Dr. Lara knows first-hand what chronic disease can do to one's quality of life, which is why she is passionate about disease prevention and reversing disease. As a wife and mother, she knows how much women tend to over commit and focus least on their own personal health. This is why Dr. Lara reaches out to women and empowers them to take control of their life and health, so they can build healthier and happier families by engaging all members of the family. She does so by addressing the mind, body and spirit through healthy lifestyle changes.

Dr. Lara is a member of Arizona Naturopathic Medical Association (AzNMA), American Association of Naturopathic Physicians (AANP), and Pediatric Association of Naturopathic Physicians (PedANP). Dr. Lara is an advocate for her patients and an advocate to bring forth a new wave of medicine that has a focus on patient centered care while using a natural and holistic approach.

About Ana's Company
Raíces Naturopathic Medical Center, PLLC
Medical Practice
www.raicesndmedcenter.com

You Are the Engine to Make Your Dreams Come True

DARRYL A. LASKER
Published Author • Founder • CEO

How I Got My Start

I didn't start to gamble until I was forty-three years old. That's through twenty plus years of being a father, fifteen years of being a husband, and twenty-one years of being a soldier in the U.S. Army. My wife, at the time, took me to a casino with her, and guess what. I won $1800! I guess that made me subconsciously believe it was easy to win and that I was likely to win every time I went. Needless to say, I've been to casinos hundreds more times since then, and I've discovered that it isn't easy to win. In fact, you're almost guaranteed to lose in my opinion.

Throughout my years of gambling, I've observed my patterns, those of the people with whom I've gambled, and those to whom I've spoken or watched from a distance. As I watched and observed, I came to a conclusion that gamblers are crazy! Not literally, but we have our crazy superstitions. Whether it's "Don't play with your player's card" or "Always bet on black" or "The machine in the corner really likes me," many of us believe we have some type of system.

On some of my drives home, I've pondered the choices that I made at the casinos and sometimes all I could do was laugh at myself and shake my head. I found myself laughing, but I also thought even more about those for whom this was no laughing matter. I thought about the many recreational gamblers whom I've seen time and time again, looking depressed, lingering at a casino, even when all of their funds have been depleted. I remember an older lady coming to watch me at a slot machine and offer commentary as I played. But she was not just being friendly; she actually began to tell me how much money she had put into the machine and that she just knew I would win back "our" money.

The places I've see this type of behavior have usually been in rural, southern locations that have a casino or a strip of casinos along the Mississippi Delta, although though this is likely the case in other places as well. I bring this up because although I can afford to have gambling as a hobby, many in these impoverished locations cannot.

Seeing this behavior at several locations got me thinking and wondering how many of these folks, seeking to better financial circumstances for themselves and their families, had gambling addictions or were teetering with that. And then, I began to just think of gambling addiction as a whole and how many people across the world have fallen victim to it. I saw a video where a man was a millionaire with a family and fell victim to a gambling disorder and lost everything.

So, at the age of fifty-four, I decided to make t-shirts that expressed some of the silly thoughts in my head about gambling, feeling that other gamblers must be having these same thoughts. I would do it in a humorous way with a loveable character to make people take notice and laugh at themselves rather than be offended. So, there I was, ten years removed from when I took that first gamble at the casino and won, taking another gamble into the business world and, of course, not sure if I'd win or not.

My Advice to Aspiring Business Owners and Entrepreneurs
As I entered the business, I had no idea what to expect. I began to look into people who were in the t-shirt business whether that was designing them with graphics or the actually printing of them. I started to hear the term print-on-demand, which is apparently a very popular way to sell t-shirts these days, especially if you don't own a printing company or equipment. I was Googling, looking at YouTube videos, asking questions—you name it! I found out that Amazon was a player in the print-on-demand industry and knew it as a reputable company. So, I figured I would sell my concepts to Amazon and sit back and let the money roll in. Little did I know that gathering all of this information was only a small beginning in the business world—very small.

Since that initial thought process, I have had to connect with graphic designers, t-shirt models, webpage designers, business consultants, trademark lawyers, social media experts, tax accountants. social media influencers, video animation producers, and the process continues.

So, my biggest piece of advice would be to go for your dreams while also understanding that YOU are the engine to make them come true. Amazon may be a place to market, print, and distribute my designs, but I have to be the one driving interest toward my product and ensuring the success of my business. "Nothing can replace hard work" may sound cliché, but nothing is truer.

Please realize that researching the field you want to enter into, making connections with those who are producing in the field and those outside the field whom you need to produce your product or service, and setting up legal and financial parameters in which to operate will all be critical to your success.

About Darryl

I am a native Arkansan. I have travelled to thirty U.S. States and the countries of Turkey and Canada. I am a twenty-one-year United States Veteran and hold several honors showcasing my dedication to creating public value in the United States. In 2018, I earned my master's degree summa cum laude, 2017 Director's ICARE Award - Veterans' Wait Times Project, 2016 Winner

VHA Employee Innovation Competition, 2019-2009 Individual Performance Cash Incentive Awards, 2012 RCS South Central Region 3B "Above and Beyond" Certificate of Recognition, 2011 Federal Executive Association of Arkansas Employee of the Year Award, and the 2010 Special Contribution Award for Exceptional Performance. My areas of expertise are human resources, employment services, veterans programs, community outreach, and administration.

I am the father of three and grandfather of three. In my spare time, I enjoy travelling, exploring new cultures, writing poetry, a variety of music, and most sports. As I get into my seasoned years, I am learning to embrace the concept of self-care, and I encourage all (yes, including millennials) to do the same. I am a recreational gambler, and I am passionate about supporting gamblers of all types to help integrate social responsibility interventions to eradicate problem gambling as well as support the gambling industry by empowering all gamblers everywhere to Please Use Gambling Sense (P.U.G.S).

About Darryl's Company
Dashry Creations LLC
An e-commerce business that sells t-shirts, sweatshirts, hoodies, and other designs
www.dashrycreations.com

Do What Fulfills You

SCOTT LEEPER

Executive Leadership and Culture Coach

How I Got My Start

I started my business as a coach after experiencing multiple life-altering challenges. As an executive coach, I focus on shifting perspective about challenges. I believe life's challenges are meant to make us stronger. They provide gifts and blessings that we would not have obtained if we remained comfortable and unchallenged. These personal and professional challenges are directly linked to leadership and culture within the organization. If one is faltering, the other three falter as well. As one grows, the other three grow as well.

Previously, I went through many challenges—personally and professionally. At the time, I believed these challenges were happening to me rather than for me. Little did I know, these massive challenges would be the prescription needed to shift the trajectory of my life, sending me and my family to levels of success—physically, psychologically, and financially. My wealth in family would skyrocket.

After these challenges forced me to take a different path, other than the military. I would eventually become a personal trainer. While I was a trainer, I had a revolving door of clientele and thought I was the sole cause of this. While I'm sure there are plenty of things I could have done differently to better empower my clientele, it became clear to me why I had this revolving door. Motivation!

I had the realization that my clients came to me motivated, which was not a bad thing at the onset. However, my clients were not switching their motivation to dedication, consistency, and discipline. Motivation has a short shelf life. It is fleeting and not sustainable. In my experience as a personal trainer, in several instances, once my clients' session packages were complete, they stopped showing up at the gym entirely. This was a clear indication that the shift to being consistent, disciplined, and dedicated to a healthy lifestyle was not established.

Shortly thereafter, a second realization came to mind. My next step would be to become a life coach. With that thought process, I immediately began coursework to become a health and life coach. After completion, I experimented with a few niches, but executive leadership and culture coaching quickly became my passion. As I developed as a coach, I understood where I could be most effective—with the growth of companies.

You'll see my story is closely related to my work with organizations. I was that individual who allowed my personal challenges to completely derail my career as a United States Marine. I lived in victimhood and believed my challenges were burdens rather than gifts.

Now I work with organizations' leadership teams to shift their perspectives about personal and professional challenges. The old saying, "Leave home at home and work at work," does not work. It's been attempted for generations. Some say it works. Most will agree it does not. So why doesn't it work? Our personal and professional lives are integral parts of our being. If we are dealing with a personal challenge, it will affect our professional life. Additionally, we can become toxic individuals with whom to work or toxic leaders, which will negatively impact the culture of our organization.

For example, if we are dealing with deeply rooted personal challenges, such as a death in the family, we might not cope well or know how to cope. This was the case for me. Eventually, it can and will start to affect other areas of our lives, such as our professions. Our work ethic might start to wane, we might become toxic leaders, and we might burn out or just not be present in our work at all.

At the same time, if we are experiencing challenges at work, such as being tasked with growing a positive work culture, feeling deadlines looming, or numbers still not reflecting a growing bottom line, this can negatively affect our personal lives. We could lose sleep, fight with our spouse, engage in extramarital affairs, engage in substance abuse, or constantly yell at our children or worse.

So, the answer is to combine these challenges into a coaching sequence and blend them with leadership and culture growth. By shifting our perspective about these challenges, we can view them from a more positive light. We can start to get curious about the challenges and ask ourselves, "What good can come out of this challenge?" or "How can I grow stronger as a result of this challenge?" This was something I had to do for myself. After being forced out of the military and fired from multiple civilian jobs, it became clear. My outlook on my current situation and challenges needed a big shift. That shift was simple but not easy. As self-development author Wayne Dyer once stated, "Change the way you look at things and the things you look at will change."

My Advice to Aspiring Business Owners and Entrepreneurs

In today's day and age, we are overwhelmed with "success" on social media. The biggest piece of advice I could suggest is to protect yourself from compare and despair. It does not take much to scroll through social media and find the latest guru with the nice car, big mansion, stacks of cash, and a "successful" business. There is no overnight success. Success is not a straight path upward. And success may not be as complete for people working outside of what fulfills them!

If you are ready to start your own business, you might need to become an hour-preneur for the first couple of years as you build your brand. Just jumping in and working for yourself might be possible for some, but others might need to maintain a job while they grow their business. With this said, set the goal of becoming a successful business owner, but don't expect this to happen overnight. It will take plenty of work and plenty of "overtime." Having the mindset of "I don't get paid to do that" as an entrepreneur or business owner might not get you too far. Especially in the coaching industry, cultivating relationships is a vital piece to growing a successful business. There have been plenty of times I have been intentional in going that extra mile for a prospective client, to add value to them without the expectation of anything in return.

Some might disagree with my previous statement about success not being as complete for people working outside of what fulfills them. What I mean by this is success is not just about money, but also about being fulfilled in our professions, relationships, spirituality, etcetera. People can make a lot of money doing something they hate, but the stress of doing a job that they do not enjoy can easily overpower the amount of money they are making, which will force them to find something else quickly. Success is also about doing something meaningful. It means being in a profession that you enjoy, with the understanding that your love for what you do will always outweigh any bad day that will arise. Ask yourself, "Would I enjoy doing this without getting paid?" Be patient but work. Define your own definition of success. Do what fulfills you.

About Scott

 Scott Leeper is an executive coach, inspirational speaker, and author, who lives in Indiana, with his wife, Ashley, and son, Jaxson. Scott served in the United States Marine Corps from 2001 to 2014, where he served as a heavy equipment operator for the first nine years of his service. In 2009, he became a Marine criminal investigator until he left the Marine Corps in 2014.

In 2012, Scott made the tough decision to take his father, Scott Leeper, Sr., off life support and watched him pass away on May 19,

2012. Scott's father battled alcohol addiction for the majority of his adult life and it would be the addiction that would ultimately cause his demise. Scott suffered severe psychological trauma after his father's death and had to reinvent himself after leaving the Marine Corps in 2014.

Due to a habit of excuses, a victim mentality, negative thinking, and an extramarital affair after his dad's death, Scott was forced out of the Marine Corps with an Other Than Honorable discharge. Although Scott was a seasoned criminal investigator with a Top Secret clearance, his law enforcement career was over. Therefore, he had to reinvent himself and learn new skills due to his negative discharge. He is happy to report that now his relationship with his wife is stronger than it ever has been!

After the end of his military service, Scott knew he wanted to help people, but did not know what that looked like for him. His first job after the military was in the staffing industry, where he would be fired less than a year later due to poor performance. His next position was with a nonprofit running multiple thrift shops in the northern Indiana region. While working for this organization, Scott conducted inspirational speeches for the men in the rehabilitation center that the organization funded. During his speeches, Scott spoke to men with various levels of addiction, without sugarcoating the realities of addiction. After the speeches, men told Scott that he spoke to them on a level that nobody had ever spoken to them on. Soon the rehabilitation center closed, and Scott found himself unfulfilled and on the job search again.

During a third job working in an office, Scott began competing in bodybuilding competitions, and, within a year, left that organization to become a certified personal trainer. As a trainer, Scott worked tirelessly to help people get the physical results they were looking for. However, Scott suffered a revolving door of clients. He began to understand the missing link. Scott understood that unless his clients made a psychological shift to consistency and a dedication to healthy habits and healthy lifestyles, their motivation would soon disappear. Once the motivation to be healthy was gone, the client stopped showing up for themselves, every time.

With this realization in mind, Scott received four certifications for health and life coaching. Scott is now the owner/operator of Mind Muscle Strength where he coaches mid-level leadership to C-suit/ownership of organizations on bridging the gap between personal and professional challenges, improving leadership skills and developing a stronger culture within their respective organizations. Scott believes that the saying, "Leave home at home and work at work," is wrong and will make a person's personal and professional lives worse. In his coaching, Scott works with people on shifting their perspectives about their personal challenges, to view them as gifts rather than burdens. He does this by calling on his own experiences and sharing his stories in a way that shows resulting strength and growth. Then he utilizes a combination of empathy, intuition, and tough love to help the individual navigate through those challenges. After working through personal challenges, he focuses on professional challenges with the individual. This creates a no-lose scenario for individuals and their organizations. By working together to navigate personal and professional challenges, improve leadership skills, and develop a stronger culture, the organization, as a whole, benefits greatly.

Scott is the coauthor of the book *Drowning in Addiction: Sink or Swim,* where the authors discuss their challenges about addiction, as the addict or the family member. The mission of the book is to start a movement to Recover Out Loud. This book can also be utilized as a resource for people to gain a perspective about becoming a much stronger person, as a result of their challenges. Scott facilitates a veteran mentoring group on Facebook title Vets Mentoring Vets as well as an in-person mentoring group titled Level Up in northern Indiana.

Scott firmly believes all the challenges he faced and continues to face are making him stronger and happened for a reason. He believes he would not be where he is now, if it were not for his challenges and how he has learned to view them.

About Scott's Company

Mind Muscle Strength, LLC
Executive Leadership and Culture Coaching
www.mindmusclestrength.com

Never Stop

BILAL ABDUS LIGGINS
President

How I Got My Start

A greater understanding of what it means to create generational wealth prompted me to start my business. While I was in my last semester of college finishing my undergraduate degree in advertising, I had what most would call an enlightenment. At the time I was facing the realization that my football career was coming to an end. I had a hard time envisioning a life without football. My plans for success had always included first going to the National Football League (NFL).

While on spring break, during a conversation with my mother regarding her childhood, I had a spiritual experience that would change my life forever. My mother had an extremely tough childhood. I had heard stories of her running away from home to escape abuse before, but that time I felt as though I was there with her. At that moment, my mind began to identify with all the stories I had ever heard of anguish, revolution, and triumph. It's possible that because I was going through my own defining moment, I was able to identify with moments that had defined others.

God showed me that there is more to the shallow view of life I had been living. I was also reminded of my love for business and people. Since I was a child, I have always loved creating and selling products. One of the first books I read after my enlightenment was *The Presentation Secrets of Steve Jobs* by Carmine Gallo. The thing that stuck with me most from that book was Steve's attention to detail while presenting. As an advertising major, I respected Jobs's ability to grasp the audience's attention and keep it.

After spring break, I returned to the University of Idaho to finish obtaining my degree. I had been having the worst semester of my college campaign. Losing football had gotten to my head, and I was failing most classes and lucky to have a D in others. Thanks to my deeper understanding of purpose, I turned my act around and studied my way to a B+ average before walking across the stage on graduation day. I hugged my mother that day and I knew that our lives had changed because of those defining moments.

I saw a lot of myself in Steve Jobs. He was a man who believed in his ideas for the future that we now live in. He wasn't extremely technologically savvy but he chose technology as the industry to create his future. Steve had the ability to get the best work out of each individual he worked with. When I returned home. I began brainstorming ideas for apps and technology that would change the world. I planned to enter the advertising industry to gain knowledge that I could apply to my own business when the time came. In 2015, I got the idea for an app that would show users events, parties, and concerts that were happening live. That year I founded DRAKO apps and began building WhosCROWDED.

My Advice to Aspiring Business Owners and Entrepreneurs

Never stop. To anyone wanting to start a business, never stop your mission. I hope your road is easy, but I doubt it will be. Remember everything is perception. Outcomes that seem bad in the present might be great in the long term. I have experienced years where progress seemed stagnant and business parttners weren't ideal. These deficiencies never stopped me from working toward a positive outcome. Sometimes your work might feel obsolete, but every step forward, no matter the distance, is one step closer to your dream. There is some magic in continuous work. Your spirit and the universe manifest your dream using the energy you put toward it.

You will be tested. Before you start your journey, I ask that you take time to examine your reason. I have found that if your reason isn't great enough, you won't continue the mission. Anything you do in life is going to include good times and hard times. Everyone loves the good times, but champions are made during hard times. I believe to continue fighting every day, people must be passionate about their business. Passion can come from different aspects of the business, but it must be present. You should be passionate enough to do the business if there were no money involved.

Somehow positive outcomes tend to find you when you continue working toward your dream. The wrong partners become the perfect partners. Progress begins to speed up. Your dream becomes your reality. The pact you make with yourself in the beginning is what keeps you taking steps no matter the distance.

About Bilal

Bilal Abdus Liggins grew up in Tacoma, Washington, a subcity of Seattle, the youngest of seven children. His father worked as a salesman and did well for himself financially for the majority of Bilal's adolescent life. His mother did not have to work but did from time to time, making sure she had her own money to buy the things she enjoyed. His grandfather was a retired sergeant major of the United States Army and had fought in two major wars. He was a hometown hero originally from Norlina, North Carolina, and moved his family to the Northwest after being stationed outside Seattle.

Bilal believes his upbringing had a foundation of discipline because of a standard his grandfather set. All Bilal's uncles had followed in his grandfather's footsteps and joined the military. Bilal's father was the only son who did not choose that route. Bilal began playing football at the age of twelve. By the time he was a high school junior, he was a star on the field and was receiving recruiting letters from colleges all over the nation. Coaches were flying into town to have dinner with him. At that time, he felt as though his future was sealed and he would be joining the NFL by the time he turned twenty-two. He wanted to study medicine and ultimately become a doctor but wasn't willing to put in the eight-plus years. On national signing day, he signed with the University of Idaho and planned to study marketing. The university is one of the top ten business schools in the United States and home to the J. A. Albertson Building, which houses the College of Business and Economics.

Those college years presented some of the greatest challenges. His football team had a habit of losing. He uses the word "habit" because he believes you can develop a habit of success or failure. In high school, the team had developed a habit of winning. Winning was to be expected and the only question they had was how much they would win by. The college team had accepted failure. The coaches fed into college football politics and allowed an acceptance of mediocrity to exist in the team. During those years, Bilal learned to be patient and work hard.

The advertising classes awoke a love for school that he had not known. Advertising is the perfect mixture of art, psychology, and business. These classes became an escape from a reality that wasn't going his way. He began to dream about a future where he could bring his ideas to life and show them to the world. During his senior year, he chose to forfeit his last year of football eligibility. He stepped out in faith and followed his heart. When he received his advertising degree from the University of Idaho, he left the campus with no plans to return until he reached success.

In the years following college, Bilal had two children. While building his dream, he struggled with homelessness, and for a period of time, he bounced from hotel to motel with his family; but during those times, he continued to build his business. He would take business calls in the business office of many hotels. Bilal doesn't expect everyone to endure the struggles he encountered, but he does believe they should never stop.

About Bilal's Company

DRAKO Apps Holding Company
Software
www.whoscrowded.com

Persevere Despite the Obstacles

DIAMONIQUE LUNDY
Serial Entrepreneur

How I Got My Start

I have three businesses, but I initially started my first business, Origin Elite®, out of mental necessity. My job in pharmaceuticals was rigid, stifling, and uninspiring, so I found an outlet through my side hustle. I blogged about different fashion or pop culture topics related to hip hop and high street fashion. I decided to create clothes for my audience—what I like to call polished, prep aesthetic with an urban flair. This career path was definitely predestined because after my first fashion show, opportunities after opportunities began to flow. I began styling for a local girl group and was even asked to be the stylist for a female newscaster. Blogging and fashion design was so exhilarating and natural.

My whole life I was told I was the "nose-in-book, practical" girl. When I tapped into my creative side, I felt most alive. It sounds like a cliché, but once you have found your passion, you do not mind working the extra hours and pushing yourself outside your comfort zone to allow your company to grow. However, like many new business owners, the ups were followed by some lows. I was laid off from my pharmaceutical job a couple of months after starting my new business. This defining moment was truly a bittersweet situation. Although I loved my side hustle and could have benefitted from the extra time, my business was not yet profitable. The loss of my job also meant the loss of the main source of funding my passion. Honestly, I fell into a rut for a couple of months and let go of a lot of great prospects.

One lesson I have learned from being a "child of the Great Recession" is to persevere. I saw many bleak times in my life as my dad, the main breadwinner, lost his job in 2008. My family and I were homeless for a couple of years. I realized that despite my current condition, after allowing myself to process my feelings, I had to get back to my first love. Starting my own business gave me a taste of the possibilities of financial freedom. It was like an addiction. I could not go back to working under someone else.

This downtime birthed another company, WEALTTH Social®. I remembered how alone I felt when I was unemployed and wanted to create a platform that would allow people to connect offline. A year later, after going back to school, I started my soul food restaurant, SoLo's Food®. I studied nutrition and was appalled by the health disparities that people of color face. This prompted me to find a solution to this problem by creating a fast food restaurant that provided healthful comfort food. Initially, starting a business stemmed from a means to escape but blossomed into a journey where I am fulfilling my purpose by contributing to society.

My Advice to Aspiring Business Owners and Entrepreneurs

Like actor Shia LeBeouf so elegantly stated in his motivational clip, "Just do it!" So many people wait around for the perfect time, the perfect business partner, family, or friends to accept their unique vision, or some other excuse. I say "excuse" because you are the creator of your destiny. If you believe you cannot do it, you will not. This logic also works the other way around. If you believe you can do it, you will. That is not to say starting your own business will not be intimidating or that it will be a walk in the park.

I have found that the most successful business owners are those who push past others' expectations and personal failings. When I realized that my strengths and my shortcomings were what I needed to make my companies lucrative, I became a successful business owner. Contrary to popular belief, starting a business is not for those who are high risk or hate unconventional jobs. I believe the best business owners are those who remove themselves from conditions lacking purpose and progress and provide those two qualities to others. Business owners are not super-smart or crazy-organized, but they are those who persevere despite the obstacles. Yes, you must do your research about your product and work to get your product to your customers, but the determining factor of a successful business is the resilience and endurance of the owner. Business, as with life, is a marathon, not a sprint.

About Diamonique

Diamonique Lundy is a serial entrepreneur and rising economic developer. After graduating with a biology degree, she entered the pharmaceutical industry. However, passions have a way of calling their owners and she was drawn to fashion. She started the blog stlundyurbandesigns.com at the beginning of 2017. This blog was the first of its kind, as it highlighted women of color who embodied a polished, hip hop style. She rolled out her clothing line three months later and it exploded.

Diamonique was recruited to head local fashion shows, style up-and-coming artists, and a newscaster, all while working a full-time job as a pharmaceutical engineer. Unexpectedly, but fortunately, she was let go from her pharmaceutical job. Facing what she deemed failure, Diamonique tapped into her well-exercised drive. What followed was the step into her life's career. The next two years would see the reinvention of St. Lundy Urban Designs into Origin Elite®, the creation of social media juggernaut, WEALTTH Social®, and innovative soul food restaurant, SoLo's Food®. Above all this success, Diamonique still credits uplifting people like herself, those who feel stuck in a career or lifestyle, as her greatest responsibility and business.

Diamonique was born in Newark, New Jersey, and raised in the neighboring town of South Orange. She returned to Newark, specifically her grandmother's home, after the financial events of

2007–2009 transpired. She likes to proudly call herself a "child of the Great Recession," which she defines as the tenacious spirit of over six million people hit the worse during those desperate times. She credits that time as the quickening process that made her into the determined businesswoman she has become.

About Diamonique's Company

Retail, Online High Street Fashion Line Technology, Social Media Company, Food/Hospitality, Soul Food Restaurant
www.solosfood.com

Find the Opportunity in Adversity

KEVIN L. MAEVERS

Expert in Community Revitalization and Economic Development

Micro-preneur • Author • Podcaster • Keynote Speaker

How I Got My Start

Like many small business owners, I grew up with a dad who wanted more from life than what a salary could provide. His desire to provide opportunity and prosperity to my mother and me drove him to leave the comfort of the family farm in southeast Missouri and travel over eighteen hundred miles west to Southern California to take part in the booming aerospace and engineering industry.

As I was growing up, I had the chance to learn at my dad's side while he went through the learning curve of several different startups. The startups included a small vending machine route, roller skating rink, and a general contracting firm. With each new venture, both Dad and I learned from the school of hard work and experience while both of us simultaneously went to school. Dad was studying civil engineering and earning his bachelor's degree while I was just doing my best to make it through high school. Following graduation, I could not wait to open my own business. I spent most of my time eating, drinking, sleeping, dreaming, and planning to be a business owner. I craved the excitement and freedom that I associated with entrepreneurship and being my own boss.

What I did not realize, until much later in my career, was that my dad was not instilling in me just a burning desire for business ownership and entrepreneurship. He was simultaneously instilling a sense of personal pride, accomplishment, ethical principles, morals, values, critical thinking, sound judgment, creativity, innovation, problem-solving ability, and a competitive desire that would make me unhappy in any form of traditional employment. It did not matter how big my salary and bonus plan grew or whether the firm gave me full control over the office, department, or division. If there was someone else calling the shots, then most likely, I was going to be unhappy.

Eventually, the reality that I was not the final decision-maker would sink in, and my inability within traditional employment to make quick, necessary, business decisions without having to obtain approval from someone else would begin to eat away at me. But perhaps the issue that drove me straight into the warm embrace of entrepreneurship was having members of upper management at two different firms ask me to perform duties that were directly in conflict with my moral and ethical values. In one situation, I was asked to reduce the staffing complement at my office so that the work being performed could be shifted to an underperforming office. The rationale that I was given was that these underperforming individuals had been hired by the firm prior to my team, so it was "last hired, first fired" even though my entire team was performing well against the production goals for the office.

In the second incidence, I was told by upper management that I was not able to terminate the employment of two individuals who had blatantly violated sexual harassment guidelines, timecard reporting requirements, and were either incapable or unwilling to meet productivity and performance goals. It was this second incident, after I had already put upper management on notice that these two individuals were going to cost the firm the ability to pay end-of-year bonuses (due to nonperformance issues) and the alerting the human resources manager that the firm was in jeopardy of being sued for harassment, that I just could not take it anymore.

I resigned my position and, with the full blessings of my wife, I jumped into micro-preneurship as a community and economic development consultant. There was no looking back now. I gathered everything I had learned about being a small business owner; created a business name, logo, and marketing materials; and let the world know that I was open for business. The first sixty days was absolutely terrifying. While I had no doubts about my talent or ability in my field of expertise, I had no idea if my message was getting to the right people. But I will never forget the morning, near the end of the second month of my entrepreneurial journey, that the phone rang. It was a former client. The first words I heard were, "Kevin, please tell me that you're available. I need your help with a major problem on my project, and I need your help today!"

My Advice to Aspiring Business Owners and Entrepreneurs

Over the course of my career, I have read hundreds of books on business, entrepreneurship, leadership, and American history. While each book I have read, each podcast I have listened to, and each lecture I have attended has yielded some small piece of knowledge or advice that has proven useful, I learned the most important piece of entrepreneurial advice from reading a biography of Benjamin Franklin. The most important personality trait that an entrepreneur must possess to be successful is the ability to embrace adversity.

It does not matter what you call your problems. Some people refer to problems as difficulties; others refer to them as misfortunes. Many just call it bad luck. Regardless of what you call it, every entrepreneur faces adversity. Adversity comes in many forms. Economic adversity may take the form of a recession or a new competitor. Regulatory adversity may come in the form of new laws, ordinances, or regulations. Technological advancement, changing social demographics, or environmental concerns can all cause an entrepreneur to question his/her commitment to the cause of self-employment. Yet contained within every professional challenge and adverse situation is the opportunity for even greater prosperity. This is especially true of the challenges that come with economic recessions.

Two of the largest and most powerful firms in the world were both founded when the United States was deeply mired in the recession of the 1970s. Bill Gates and Paul Allen founded Microsoft in 1975. Steve Jobs and his partner Steve Wozniak founded Apple in 1976. From extremely humble beginnings and on a shoestring budget, both these firms have grown, prospered, and now have a global impact that has created thousands of other companies and an untold number of millionaires and billionaires. Had Gates and Allen or Jobs and Wozniak listened to the critics and the naysayers—those who said that their ideas would never amount to anything—or believed that the timing was bad or that there was no market for those silly electronic computing machines, the world would be a much less prosperous place.

Find the opportunity in adversity. Embrace it. Make it your own. Come up with a plan to deliver products and services in a new, innovative way Then press on with the passion and knowledge that you too are following a path that can lead to tremendous prosperity for yourself and for those who are willing to come along with you.

If you are currently struggling with any type of adversity in your life, it might help to remember the words of Calvin Coolidge, the thirtieth President of the United States of America: "Nothing in the world can take the place of **persistence**. Talent will not; nothing is more common than unsuccessful men with talent. Genius will not; unrewarded genius is almost a proverb. Education will not; the world is full of educated derelicts. **Persistence** and determination alone are omnipotent. The slogan **'Press On'** has solved and always will solve the problems of the human race."

About Kevin

Kevin L. Maevers was born in the small town of Cape Girardeau, Missouri. He is the son of a seventh-generation Missouri farmer. But it was his father's desire for a better life for Kevin and his mother that pushed his dad to pick up everything and head west to California. Jake Maevers, Kevin's father, had an entrepreneurial spirit that he passed on to his son early in life. While Jake was learning land surveying and civil engineering, Kevin was growing his newspaper delivery route and helping his dad on weekends to clean, maintain, and restock the hundreds of small candy and peanut vending machines that his dad owned.

When Kevin was fourteen, his dad announced to the family that he had quit his job and had purchased the local roller-skating rink. The skating rink had sat vacant for several years and was a complete mess, but Jake wanted to be open for the summer; so they had ninety days to get things repaired and ready for opening day. It was during the five years that Jake owned and operated the A.V. Skateway that Kevin fell in love with everything about being a small business owner. Kevin worked every job at the skating rink—scrubbing floors and toilets, painting graphics on the walls, cleaning and servicing the roller skates, snack bar attendant, DJ booth announcer, and skating session manager. These experiences and skills he learned while working with his dad at the A.V. Skateway translated into many more opportunities in food service management, real estate, radio, television, and voiceover work.

It wasn't all work for Kevin; he was still going to high school and taking advantage of both the educational opportunities and the vocational classes that were available. Most important, Kevin had inherited his dad's love of civil engineering and architectural design. At sixteen, Kevin secured a job as a design/draftsman with a local firm. By nineteen, Kevin had moved to a different firm and was part of a small startup. But by his twentieth birthday, Kevin knew that he was never going to be completely satisfied unless he was in a position where he could be his own boss.

Finally, the opportunity arrived while at the dinner table on Thanksgiving Day. Once again, Jake announced he was ready to make a move back into self-employment. He had grown tired of making the daily two-hour commute to work for a municipal agency near Los Angeles. Kevin and Kent, Kevin's younger brother, both chimed in and said they were also ready because both Kevin and Kent felt undervalued by the owners of the small companies where they worked at the time. The challenges and opportunities were discussed for a couple of hours and then Jake finally said, "If we're so smart, why don't we do it ourselves?"

Thus began an entrepreneurial journey that has lasted for over thirty years. Not every venture has been successful, and occasionally the timing was just plain awful. However, when you build something of your own, there is no other feeling like it. Over the course of his entrepreneurial career, Kevin has had the opportunity to create dozens of good-paying jobs for others. Many of the people who have worked for him went on to other opportunities where they are now well-paid and well-respected professionals in the urban planning, civil engineering, and environmental science fields.

Kevin would be lying to you if he said that success was easy or that the days are always filled with sunshine and rainbows. However, his strong commitment to excellence and adherence to his personal philosophy to "press on!" has seen him through the difficult times and kept him focused on the possibilities that dawn with every new day.

For the past ten years, Kevin has owned and operated Arivitas Strategies from his home office in Southern California. He is a recognized expert in community development and downtown revitalization, economic development, and affordable housing strategies. His ability to envision opportunities where others only see obstacles then to apply practical and time-tested techniques to achieve a positive outcome has given him a high level of professional credibility with the public and private sectors.

Responding to the economic uncertainty of early 2020, Kevin decided to take positive action to support and promote micro-preneurship. He relaunched his professional brand, K.L.Maevers & Company, with a new mission to use his 30+ years of business and 10+ years of teaching experience to work directly with small and micro-business owners to find innovative ways to provide goods and services in a post-COVID-19 economy. Then, Kevin went further and launched the Academy of Leadership and Micro-preneurial Innovation (ALMI). The ALMI uses the latest technology platforms to deliver timely and relevant information to those who aspire to be micro-preneurs but need additional training and practical advice before making the investment in their future.

About Kevin's Companies
K.L.Maevers & Company
Innovative small and micro-business consulting services designed to take your company to the next level of success
Maevers.biz

Academy of Leadership and Micro-preneurial Innovation
Small group workshops to advance the micro-preneurial spirit and prepare the micro-business owner for success and prosperity.
ALMI.academy

Arivitas Strategies, LLC
Innovative Strategies for Community Revitalization, Affordable Housing, Economic Development, and Environmental Stewardship
arivitas.com

Go for It!

PATTI LYNN MAMALIS
Owner Creator of Power word Postcards

How I Got My Start

I started creating Power word Postcards in 1995. I was going through a difficult divorce, was a mother of four boys, and a full-time kindergarten teacher. The divorce took a toll on me emotionally. I started channeling my inner kindergarten teacher and started cutting words out of magazines and gluing them together in word collages with different themes. Then I had the cards printed and started mailing them to my friends and family members. I got a great deal of joy creating these cards, mailing them to my friends and family, and even mailing them to myself because I am worth a stamp. So I became a hobbypreneur.

Because the response and feedback were so positive about Power word Postcards, I kept creating different designs. I transitioned to the next step. a wanna-be-preneur. I wanted to start getting the word out. I started being a vendor at farmers' markets, craft fairs, and church boutiques. How could I possibly do this while being a single mom and a full-time teacher? The desire to make this an official business was strong.

I got in my own way and the quote, "If you think you can, or if you think you can't—you're right," became my mantra I said over and over again. I was not going to say "I can't" anymore. I knew in my heart that Power word Postcards was my calling and what I was truly supposed to be doing. The joy that I provide with an amazing selection of inspirational motivational postcards and the service I provide with a handwritten message is exactly what keeps me moving forward and believing in myself.

In December 2014, I took the biggest leap of faith that I could have possibly imagined becoming a full-fledged entrepreneur. I retired from teaching kindergarten after twenty-seven years. This allowed me to focus my attention and my energy and put everything into Power word Postcards. I rented office space, I invested in inventory, I attended (and still do) many networking events, and I am involved with a variety of networking groups. I market, I sell, I am an entrepreneur.

My nine-to-five job looks different. I follow my own time schedule, work when work needs to get done, fulfill orders as they come in, and couldn't be happier. I know I am following my dream with a product of which I am extremely proud. If you think you can or you think you can't, you're right!

My Advice to Aspiring Business Owners and Entrepreneurs
The greatest advice I can offer anyone who wants to be an entrepreneur is to go for it. If you have an idea, make it a great idea and

go for it. If you think you can do something, or if you think you can't do something, you are exactly right. So, if you have an idea and you think you can do it, then go for it. You don't have to worry about how. I will give you some advice on how to make it happen.

Start with the end in sight. Where do you want to be in ten years? Write out your big, audacious, scary goals. Goals that sound so scary they can't possibly happen or come true. Start with the end in mind and go for it. Ten-year goals, three-year goals, this-year goals, and make them all happen.

When you start on a trip, you have a map, a plan, and directions. The same is true about starting a business. Get crystal clear with your goals. Not only do you need to start with the end in sight with where you want to be in ten years, include who you want to work with. Who are the people who are the best fit for your product or service? How are you going to reach those perfect customers? What employees do you need to support you and make your company a rockstar team? Write all these answers down in your plan.

This is your road map for your journey. Also, identify your super-power. What makes you stand out from your competition? Now create systems that will work for you. The flow, the rhythm, the policies, the customer service practices, the products, and the service are the how. If you think you can, or if you think you can't—you're right.

About Patti

 Patti Lynn Mamalis is the owner and creator of Power word Postcards. She earned her bachelor's degree from Davis & Elkins College in Elkins, West Virginia, and her master's degree in education from Arizona State University in Tempe, Arizona. She lives in Tempe, Arizona with her most amazing husband and business partner, Larry. Patti has four adult sons with a daughter-in-law on the way.

Patti was a schoolteacher for twenty-seven years in the Tempe Elementary School District, teaching kindergarten all those years. Patti loves having her own business and following her dream. Her mission statement is to inspire, motivate, support, encourage, and connect. She prides herself with her product and service to do just that. Patti is active in the Chandler Chamber of Commerce, Network Together, and Power Networking Team.

Patti is just getting started in Toastmasters International, which will help in her speaking abilities for her weekly video, "Orange You Glad It's Thursday." Patti gets up early to do her "spiritual gym" routine, which includes posting the word of the day on Instagram, meditation, affirmations, journal writing, Bible reading, and prayer. Patti loves to play golf, be outside, go to movies, and eat out. She believes in the power of "snail mail" and frequently mails cards to friends, family, and business owners.

About Patti's Company

Power word Postcards

Inspire, Motivate, Support

www.powerwordpostcards.com

Find a Mentor

JOHN MAPEL
Entrepreneur • Digital Marketing Specialist

How I Got My Start

I've started several businesses, and I think they all emerged because I felt there was a need for them to exist. Almost everything I've ever done has revolved around professional services—for me that means helping people. So essentially, there were situations where I was consistently being asked for help or guidance by my contacts and peers. They trusted my advice and knew that I had the skills and experience to help them with their problems. So I took this as a sign to start marketing these services as a business.

My history as an entrepreneur has gone through several changes and developments along the way. I've founded and cofounded several businesses, including a video production company, a music studio, a kitesurfing school, a yoga school, a sports tour company, a distribution company, a health supplement company, and a birth training company. All of them originated because of some sort of need or "gap in the market," so to speak, of my environment. Some of these were successes for ten-plus years, and some only worked fairly well for a year or so before I decided to stop putting energy into them. A few are still continuing under the management of others. Regardless of which have been deemed successes or failures, I believe they were all necessary learning experiences.

Accumulatively, I realized the one thing that all these ventures shared was a need for an effective marketing strategy. In the beginning, I hired professionals to do this work for me. Then, along the way, I began to learn how to advertise and promote my businesses on my own. I became almost more interested in this aspect of my businesses than what the business entailed. So, I enrolled in further courses and mentorship programs to continue learning. I then started partnering with other companies to help consult with their marketing strategies.

Two years ago, I decided to focus my efforts on building a new company that specializes in direct response marketing services for entrepreneurs and small businesses. Entresol Agency is the result of that. Our main aim for our clients is to provide them with constant streams of client leads, develop a system to engage with them, and ultimately turn them into raving fan customers. I'm proud of this work, because I feel like it helps both sides (the business and the customer) find exactly the product or service they are looking for, while utilizing an influential, educative process, which is characteristic of good direct response marketing.

My Advice to Aspiring Business Owners and Entrepreneurs
Find a mentor. This is definitely the most important advice I can give someone who's just starting out. When you have a business (and

you're most likely going to start managing it yourself for the first year or so), you're going to run into all sorts of challenges you never would have imagined. You need someone who's been there to help point the way and guide you through difficulties. Spending all the time and effort figuring out how to solve the problems yourself is probably going to drive you crazy and your business could fall apart—not the result we are wanting from having our own business. I think it's definitely worth considering working for someone as an apprentice, for three to six months, to get some inside understanding of the nuances what come with that business.

Another idea is if there's someone that you know/trust who is successful in the business you'd like to be in, tell them your plan, and offer to pay them for biweekly consultations (or phone calls if they're not local) to help answer your questions as you're building your business. Just remember, in both situations, that you could be seen as competition by the business or person you're getting advice from, so keep in mind that you might want to (respectfully) start your business activities in a location where you're not competition. You could even suggest to your mentor that you start your business as an extension of theirs in a new location—mutual benefit!

If you can't find someone within your community who you can work for or get advice, consider going online and investing in a course to learn to do what you want. I'm a big fan of online courses! Many of them only cost a few hundred dollars, and they will often offer ongoing personalized support from the experts, so you'll always feel like someone's got your back. If you decide to invest in one of these programs, spend a good amount of time researching it and weighing its strengths and weaknesses compared to other courses. Once you decide on which option you want to support you as you go along with your business endeavor, follow through with this guidance and training. It'll benefit you greatly in the long run!

About John

John Mapel was born and raised in Columbus, Georgia. He grew up with a lot of support from his parents to always learn and do new things—sports, music, academics. Because of this, he was instilled with driving curiosity about the world, people, and spirituality. John went to the Savannah College of Art and Design, with a music scholarship, and studied film and sound design.

During his time at college, John and a friend won a national song writing contest. With that money, they started a business as a music studio. They had an intense entrepreneurial drive and, a couple of years later, they honed their passions and started other ventures—a kitesurfing school, a watersports tour operation, and a surfboard distribution company, which imported products from Europe and China.

Later, John moved to Brooklyn, New York, and worked in music production and performance for three years, producing two albums with his girlfriend and performing in the US and Europe with their band.

Their son was born in 2018 in Switzerland. Since then, they've relocated to Barcelona, Spain, where John teaches English to business professionals, continues to play music, and works in online business endeavors, with a main focus on his digital marketing company, Entresol.

About John's Company
Entresol
Marketing and Advertising
https://entresol.agency/

Don't Overthink It

DEAH BERRY MITCHELL
Cultural Experience Curator • Food Equity Advocate • Writer

How I Got My Start

About a year prior to founding The Soul of DFW tours, I had produced the first brunch-themed festival in North Texas. It was successful from a technical perspective, but I knew I wanted to create something with more depth. I just wasn't sure what that would be. A few months had gone by, and I went on vacation. Whenever I travel (either domestically or internationally), I make it a priority to immerse myself into the local culture via tours.

At this particular moment I was having a difficult time deciding between a food tour or a history tour because I had a great appreciation for both. It was in this moment of indecision that the idea for The Soul of DFW was born. I returned home to Dallas, Texas, and immediately called my friend Dalila Thomas, a writer and producer of a local television station, to discuss the idea and invite her to help me spearhead this project. After contemplating the logistics, we decided to embark on a journey together by creating a tour that would highlight black culture.

We do this primarily by focusing on two avenues of culture: food and history. On each of our tours, we alternate between visiting black-owned restaurants for food samples of their most prized dishes and stopping by for historical sites for impromptu history lessons. For the food businesses, we are also able to meet with these entrepreneurs and hear their stories firsthand. It's amazing to hear of their challenges and successes in the food and beverage industry. It's also an opportunity for them to market to a population who might not have otherwise known about their establishments.

On the same tour, we guide the passengers into local history. Sometimes we visit historical sites that are particularly significant and discuss the impact on the city and other times we might be able to meet with local advocates who are able to share insights on how their communities have helped shape the city.

In the beginning, I wanted to offer an alternative for people looking for unique event experiences. What it has become, however, has been much more rewarding! The Soul of DFW is the premier source for educating communities about the cultural impact of black people on a local scale.

My Advice to Aspiring Business Owners and Entrepreneurs

My advice to anyone looking to start a business is simple. Don't overthink it. Obviously, you will want to do your due diligence and research to make sure it's a sound idea. But other than that, does the project speak to you? Is it an extension of you? Is this something you could see yourself doing without potentially earning a profit in the beginning? Does it scare you? If you answered yes to each of those questions, then you are more than ready.

My first entrepreneurial attempt as an adult was a few years ago after being laid-off from a job I had held for a decade. I was afraid to start something new, but I knew I had to do try. I have always enjoyed cooking and I was intrigued by food marketing, so I decided to parlay these interests into a small outdoor pop-up bistro called The Urban Brunch Co. Here I would have a few select signature dishes to be served at our local artisanal outdoor market. I researched color psychology and font designs before crafting the menu and the logo, hired a small (and outstanding) staff that was devoted to providing exceptional customer service and that believed in me 110%, and rented a commercial kitchen to prepare the foods and meet with my new team.

At that time, not many people were doing pop-ups (temporary restaurants with nonfixed operational hours), and it appealed to my noncommittal attitude at the time. My plan was to try to look for a permanent job during the work week and focus on food on the weekends. I was completely overwhelmed and exhausted, but it was a wonderful learning experience that I grew so much from in terms of my business intelligence! Much of what I learned I still apply to each of my new interests and projects. The questions I posed above are the questions I asked myself then and I ask myself now!

About Deah

Deah Berry Mitchell, a graduate of Southern Methodist University, has written for various school newspapers and magazines. After receiving her undergraduate degrees in physiology and sports marketing and a brief internship with the National Football League Super Bowl, she continued a path leading toward a professional career in sporting events. As fate would have it, an unexpected layoff forced Deah, a born teacher, to rely on her innate gifts for creating elegant meals at home and instructing others how to prepare the same. During this time, she started a pop-up outdoor eatery and used this time to hone her cooking skills by gaining an instructor position at a gourmet food and cookware retailer.

Just before receiving her master's degree in creative writing, she began researching the origins of soul food. Deah has worked professionally in the nonprofit development sector for over a decade, helping fund some subjects from higher education to health sciences. Hailing from Sherman, Texas, and like many Southern natives, she was raised in a family of traditionalists eating the foods she's researched. After moving to Houston, Texas, and gaining influences from various cultures, she began to incorporate those cooking styles into her recipes.

When she's not developing recipes, Deah, a self-proclaimed food enthusiast, speaks to communities about local food culture and food history, enjoys traveling, entertaining friends and family at home, planning events, and writing. Deah volunteers with a local Dallas nonprofit, FEED Oak Cliff, and works within the community to increase awareness of food deserts and health equity.

About Deah's Company
The Soul of DFW
Hospitality/Tourism
www.soulofdfw.com

Starting Your Business is Easy … Sticking to it is Harder

SIMONE E. MORRIS
Career/Inclusion Strategist • Speaker • Author

How I Got My Start

The decision to start a business is an easy one. What's harder is deciding to stick to your business. I know this because I've attempted it three different times, and let's just say the third time was the charm.

The first try was many moons ago. I decided I needed a side hustle and was good at graphics, so I decided to open a graphics design business. I called it Creative Ventures and I thought I was super official when my limited liability company (LLC) certificate arrived in the mail. I even had an ink stamp with my business name etched on it. It was truly exciting. I got a few clients here and there but nothing to signal a departure from corporate America. Certainly not enough revenue to sustain my lifestyle. Disappointed, I shut the LLC down.

It should be noted that because this was a side hustle business, it was easy for me to shift more of my focus back to my full-time corporate America job. There came a time when dissatisfaction reared its head. I decided to take a sabbatical and found a passion for coaching. After enrolling in 116 hours of training and twenty-five weeks of certification, I was a Certified Professional Co-Active Coach (CPCC).

For the second try, I decided to launch Simone Morris Coaching after securing additional expertise. Still not fully convinced that I could maintain this business in a full-time capacity, I hesitated but proceeded. My interests grew along the way, and I embraced my talents for photography with an expanded offering to include photography. I was willing to try multiple strategies to make it work this time. I was now maintaining different websites to reach different audiences, and it got a bit tricky and hard to handle seamlessly. The money just wasn't flowing as anticipated, and so I became disillusioned yet again. This would lead me to shut my business down for the second time. I was lucky to have a full-time job that took this journey with me, so I continued along in corporate America. As a lifelong learner, I continued to invest in myself and embraced natural aptitude testing as an opportunity for further clarity on my passion and true calling. Entrepreneurship was a part of the result, and since I had botched that multiple times, I didn't give it much credence.

My third try, in 2013, happened when the time came for me to close the chapter to my corporate America career. I was uncertain what my next chapter would be. Should it be another organization, or should it be another try at entrepreneurship? I decided to give entrepreneurship another go after multiple rejections for diversity and inclusion jobs. I struggled with low salary offers and entry-level jobs sent my way for consideration due to switching areas of expertise. It felt like my experience wasn't being valued, and so I decided to get in the driver's seat for my career. I decided I would open a business that showcased my talents. I founded Simone Morris Enterprises, LLC in 2015. Shout out to my friend, Anne, for helping me with a name that allows me to explore all my talents under the same business umbrella.

All these tries to open a business were a foundation to keep me grounded in the third try. Being an entrepreneur isn't easy, but it's fulfilling. Over time, there became a deep-seated belief in my capabilities. I got clearer about my offerings, shaving things that didn't make sense. What I liked was that it was on my terms and not allowing others to call the shots, convincing me to niche down when I wasn't ready. I wanted to be a true beacon for inclusion. I wanted to take the biggest bet on myself because I knew the rewards were unlimited. Five years later, I finally stepped into my chief executive officer (CEO) shoes for my business. Much has been learned.

My Advice to Aspiring Business Owners and Entrepreneurs

I have lots of advice to give aspiring business owners. If I had to narrow it down to just one, I would encourage them to give it a try. Don't let other people's fears squash your dreams. Give it a try, and then tweak how you want to show up based on your results. As you can see from my story, I had to tweak multiple times until I decided to go all-in as a business owner. There have been many times that I've felt like giving up, but I always remember the message from a

Women's Business Enterprise National Council (WBENC) conference where the keynote speaker said that the difference between successful people and unsuccessful people is that successful people don't give up. That message reinforced to me that I needed to stick to my third try.

Other advice I have includes investing in creating a plan for your business. I didn't understand the advice about the importance of the business plan, but it's an exercise in thinking through the viability of your business. You need to understand products/services, how you plan to make money, competition, marketing, financials, and more. My early mistake was not being super clear about my offerings and not focusing enough on revenue and tracking the true numbers of my business. Becoming a certified minority woman-owned business has provided training that has been beneficial to me in business. I would also say to earmark money to keep learning the art of being a business owner. Create an annual professional development plan where you identify what capabilities you're going to build throughout the year. Be sure to have some training that teaches you how to be a better CEO

About Simone

Simone E. Morris is the CEO of Simone Morris Enterprises, LLC, a certified minority and woman-owned business enterprise. She is an award-winning diversity and inclusion leader and a consultant and speaker committed to training women and

emerging leaders to take true leadership positions in all aspects of their lives.

Simone has a background that includes over two decades in corporate America, spanning information technology, commercial strategy, and human resources. She holds a master's degree in business administration from the University of Connecticut. Her technology background has served her well, embedding strong project management acumen that allows her to educate and create transformational results for her clients. She teaches diversity and inclusion, conscious inclusion, and project management.

Simone shares her message across various platforms, for example, Forbes, Medium, Thrive Global, Glassdoor, Leadercast, SmartRecruiters, Social Hire, Diversity Best Practices, Profiles in Diversity Journal, and BambooHR. She is the author of *Fifty-Two Tips for Owning Your Career: Practical Advice for Career Success, The Power of Owning Your Career: Winning Strategies, Tools and Tips for Creating Your Desired Career!* and *Achievement Unlocked: Strategies to Set Goals and Manifest Them.* She resides in Connecticut with her family.

About Simone's Company
Simone Morris Enterprises, LLC
Professional Services
www.simonemorrisenterprises.org

Identify What You Want and Outline Your Action Plan

RACHAEL MAZVITA NYAMWENA-SABONDO

Certified Life Coach • International Labour Organization (ILO) Trainer • Conference Speaker • Author

How I Got My Start

What motivated me to start a business was the need to have extra income. I was fully employed and a mother of four. I would always think of ideas about how to make extra income. Although my spouse and I had two salaries as a couple, it was never enough for there was a need for rentals, school fees, and food. As I was looking for money, I discovered my passion for training and I enrolled in Training of Trainers with the International Labour Organization in 2004. From there, I would do my nine-to-five job and would do part-time trainings. Each time I got part-time training jobs, I was so fulfilled and realized that this was my calling.

Personal development was of significance to me, so I obtained a bachelor's degree in management of human resources and graduated in 2006. I remember one of the exams I wrote while pregnant with my third child. The company I worked for would send me for courses in public relations, leadership, and so on. All the time, I desired to start my consultancy company. To enhance this business, I enrolled in a program to earn a master's degree in business administration and graduated in 2016. During this course, I conceived two things, my fourth child and another business idea. The idea emanated that in Zimbabwe so many people are creative and innovative but they lack the exposure and the markets.

Inga Creative was birthed to create more awareness of the work being done by creative people and to lobby for local and overseas markets. Innovativeness is seen and celebrated, but after a few years you stop hearing about that person and that idea. My desire was to have those ideas be turned into sustainable projects and businesses that would be handed over from one generation to the next. Inga Creative was registered in February 2019.

My Advice to Aspiring Business Owners and Entrepreneurs

If you want to start a business, you must identify what you want and desire. You write what you want to have and accomplish no matter if it might look impossible to achieve at the moment. You have to determine your motivation. My motivation was to leave a legacy for my children. I wanted to leave something that my great-grand-children would thank me for.

There is a need to outline your action plan about how to achieve your dream. You have to know what you want to achieve, why and how you will be able to achieve this. For me, mobilizing capital looked so big for I had a dream of having a double-story building where there would be trainings for creativity and innovation. I wanted that after the trainings people showcased their products and had sales. The idea was there from 2015, and when I thought about it, I would say, "I do not even have money to buy land."

In 2018, I attended Power Classes for Women (#PC4W) led by Anoziva Marindire. The training was for six weeks. I learned that you have to break down your goals and see what can be done this month, in six months, in one year, in five years, etc. This made me look closely at my project.

In January 2019, I attended a life coaching certification program by Blessing Duri and had to create a vision board. That's when I realized that capital was not an issue when you have a dream. In March 2019, we started the first exhibition at a place where we used without paying for the space.

About Rachael

Rachael Mazvita Nyamwena-Sabondo is a certified life coach, ILO trainer, consultant, and author. She specializes in coaching women and young people about entrepreneurship skills. Rachael is experienced in training others about "How to Start Your Business," "How to Improve Your Business," "Career Coaching," and many other issues such as emotional intelligence and self-awareness. Rachael got the

Career Coach of the Year award for 2019, second runner-up Business Coach of the Year award, and first runner-up Mentor of the Year award at the 2019 International Coaching and Mentoring Awards. Rachael is passionate about creating markets for women. She holds monthly meeting called "Creative Market" days. Her desire is to create a space where women can connect, learn together, showcase skills, and spark collaborations. Based in Harare, Zimbabwe, Rachael works closely with her clients and this has enabled her to create progressive relationships that support women on their entrepreneurial journeys.

Rachael was certified as life coach at International Coaching and Mentoring Foundation in Zimbabwe and holds a master's degree in business administration from Women's University in Africa. She also holds a bachelor's degree in management of human resources from Zimbabwe Open University. Rachael does one-on-one coaching, facilitates group sessions, leads workshops, and is an inspiring speaker. Rachael loves writing and contributes to three different entrepreneur magazines. She also likes to travel, reads widely, and is a dedicated mother of three girls and one boy.

About Rachael's Company
Inga Creative
Consultancy, Arts and Crafts

Use Your Head and Heart to Create Something to Better Our World

TISHA MARIE PELLETIER

Chief Experience Officer • Keynote Speaker • Author • Connector

How I Got My Start

I had this fantastic vision when I was attending the Walter Cronkite School of Journalism and Mass Communication at Arizona State University (ASU)—I was going to be the next Connie Chung. But, I was shown the harsh realities of the industry while in my senior year and diverted to a "safer" career path in marketing, advertising, events, and public relations.

I'll never forget when I was at my job, which was a small advertising agency. I loved my account executive role, helping clients build their businesses through traditional marketing channels and live events. It was my happy and I was damn good at it. What wasn't my happy was working in a toxic environment where the open-door policy didn't exist, women were catty, there was no room for advancement, the head honcho couldn't make a decision, and every day we didn't know if the doors were closing. It was that unpredictable. It was an awful, pit-in-your-stomach kind of feeling.

I was twenty-four at the time. Newly married, I had this sneaky suspicion that the universe was screaming at me it was time to go. I hadn't even contemplated becoming an entrepreneur this early in life. I still hadn't gotten the "real world" experience I thought I needed. Luckily, I received an opportunity from a vendor that would allow me to help his business grow and become a business owner at the same time so I wouldn't go into total freak-out mode and still have income coming in.

I was so excited to make my move. I gave my resignation. I did my due diligence. I learned what I could about being an entrepreneur. The day I quit, the vendor told me he had cold feet, backed away from our arrangement, and I was left confused and in total shock asking myself, "What the heck now?" What about the staff at the ad agency? Yep, they mostly turned their backs and made me feel like I was the smallest person in the world.

When the universe throws a curveball your way, you are faced with a major life decision. Keep letting other people control your destiny, or take the reins and control your own. My journey into entrepre- neurship started September 10, 2004, with my first company, Simply Put Marketing Communications. I was just shy of my twenty-fifth birthday and ten years earlier than I ever expected to own a business.

It was the hardest, yet best decision I've ever made to not let others design my life, but for me to do it in my time and on my own terms. Now, four businesses later, I can't get enough of being an entrepreneur, the perks that come with it (sometimes) and helping others experience the same joy and freedom I have.

My Advice to Aspiring Business Owners and Entrepreneurs

There is no greater, or a more rewarding, feeling than knowing that your head and heart created something to better the world we live in. That, my friends, is my definition of entrepreneurship.

About Tisha

Tisha Marie Pelletier is confident, witty, approachable, and authentic with a touch of badass. Tisha is the type of entrepreneur and speaker who walks the talk and rolls with the punches.

Tisha is the president and chief experience officer of Tisha Marie Enterprises, LLC, empowering entrepreneurs from startups to established businesses to help make their businesses happen through mentoring, consulting, her online courses, the Startup Entrepreneur Academy, and her special events including the Social Connect Business Happy Hour and Success over Struggle speaker panel.

Tisha is an inspirational speaker, the host of The Success Over Struggle Podcast, and a mentor at ASU Entrepreneurship +

Innovation department. In addition, she's an author. Her latest book, *What Are the Odds? A Mom Shares Her Good, Bad and What the F*ck Moments*, can be found on Amazon and Audible.

About Tisha's Company

Tisha Marie Enterprises, LLC
Business Consulting
www.tishamarie.com

Give Yourself Space and Grace

NIKI RAMIREZ

Founder • Principal Consultant

How I Got My Start

As I pull off the busy street, bustling with morning rush-hour traffic, into the university parking lot, I can see her, just a small speck in the distance. It's my mom, who was left paraplegic for life after being a passenger in a deadly car accident when she was fifteen. Yet there she is. Hoisting her wheelchair out of her car by herself so she can head in to work; a testament to her strength and ambition in the face of adversity.

When people ask me why I started my business, I share with them that I started my business in honor of my mom, and the millions of other people who are judged every day, not by what they can do or what they have achieved, but for what others believe, unknowingly, about them and their abilities. I started my business to help employers learn to carefully balance their businesses with the needs of their employees. To help them create workplaces that people love, where all employees feel valued and respected. There are other reasons that I left my corporate nine-to-five job, but this is the one that lights my fire. The reason I get up in the morning. My why.

For the past twenty years, working as an operations leader and human resources (HR) professional, I have had the privilege of having a line of sight into the most remarkable and interesting workplace situations, and the most sensitive and difficult issues that arise at work. Over the years, I have witnessed the difference that a good leader, and a solid HR foundation can make. I patiently learned alongside experienced experts and listened as they told stories about their journeys, and their paths to success and fulfillment.

In 2016, with my collective life and professional experience under my belt, and the support of my family, I was ready to strike out on my own and founded HRAnswers.org, a progressive human resources consulting firm focused on helping business leaders create clarity and consistency (and happiness!) in their organizations by designing and implementing exceptional human resources programs. In addition to helping employers learn to carefully balance their businesses with the needs of their employees, there are a few other reasons I decided to venture out on my own. I am excited to share them now!

Design a new, more flexible way to deliver support. After years of observations regarding how businesses benefitted from the support of an experienced human resources professional, I decided to pour myself into designing flexible HR-support options that scale as a business scales and supports employers as they ebb and flow with business. In addition to flexibility, I aimed to design something affordable. Most organizations do not have the $100,000 annual budget to hire a human resources professional in their business, full-time, and bundling HR support with other services, like payroll, can be extremely costly. Unlike other solutions, I wanted to provide affordable as-needed services, project support, and intensive HR consulting depending on what the client needs.

Take the burden off business leaders so they can focus on what they do best. In business, human resources activities, like writing an employee handbook or job descriptions, are often left on the back burner, understandably so. Leaders are often consumed with day-to-day operations and business development activities. HR is something that leaders "do" in response to a complaint or an issue. I've also seen HR function as a defense team. Trying to deflect and deny issues that arise on a team or in an organization. When this defensive, reactive approach is adopted, employees feel shut out and scared. Clearly, scared employees cannot do their best work. Moreover, issues in an organization do not just go away merely because one denies that they exist; oftentimes, they get worse. By founding HRAnswers.org, I aimed to redefine this, to offer leaders a flexible approach to focusing on their own goals, while having the expert support and guidance needed to develop and refine their HR programs, thereby strengthening their entire organization.

Create a positive ripple in the world. As I see it, and I know I might be biased, HR is a mighty, invisible glue that holds people together and makes all things possible. Without people, there is no business. It is my goal to design a dynamic approach to HR that helps leaders learn to focus on their people (employees) while balancing their business goals and objectives (profits and growth). Through the practice of intentional, proactive leadership in human resources, we all have the ability to positively affect employees' lives and build better communities.

My Advice to Aspiring Business Owners and Entrepreneurs

Give yourself space. When I say give yourself space, I mean "time." Take the time you need to develop your own specific, deep expertise; along with your ideas, values, and offerings. For many entrepreneurs, I've seen this process play out quickly and successfully. And for others (like me), it unfolds more slowly. My business has grown about 30 percent year over year since I left my nine-to-five job, but I've seen others in related industries grow larger, faster. I attribute my slow-but-steady growth to being methodical and thoughtful in my business, and also to my commitment to align my business with my values. I am building a business that allows my team and me to balance work and life. For example, I volunteer about twenty work days per year (and my employees are eligible for paid volunteer time each year). In addition, my family vacations a cumulative of four to six weeks each year.

Make space for on-going growth and on-going inspiration. Give yourself time to learn about aspects of business with which you are unfamiliar. For me, as an example, that is accounting. As an HR professional, accounting is not my area of expertise. In the years that I've operated my own business, I've leaned on my bookkeeper and accountant, mostly from day one to ensure that we were properly set up and running smoothly. This gave me the space that I needed to focus on forging stronger relationships with clients and creating a service and product offering that is valuable to my clients.

Before we move on from space, I want to mention how powerful it is to give yourself time and space to invest in building and nurturing your network as you approach your entrepreneurial launch. Being an entrepreneur, especially a new one, can feel lonely. In addition, you might lack funding to infuse your marketing plan but still need to get the word out about your new business. You will need to lean on your network more than you know, both for kinship and for support. Spend time building and serving your network and you cannot go wrong.

Give yourself grace. When I say give yourself grace, I mean be patient and forgiving with yourself. It is true that we are often our own worst critics. Entrepreneurs, as a group, harshly judge our own work. We are overthinkers. We stay up late considering how we can do more, do better, and do it right. We agonize over details and beat ourselves up over things that, in the end, are unlikely to harm us or our businesses.

As you venture out on your own, fellow entrepreneur, you will make mistakes. It is true that those mistakes can cost you time, money, or both. However, do not let that derail your plans or deter you from chasing your dreams, for the best lessons are found in mistakes. Our most substantial growth comes in times when we feel broken and lost. When mistakes happen, remind yourself of your why. Go back to your roots and remind yourself of your own values. Reflect, learn your lesson, and get back to work!

About Niki

Niki Ramirez is an industry expert and certified human resource professional with over twenty years of successful experience in human resources management and leadership. She is a sought-after consultant, speaker, and trainer who has taken what she learned in Fortune 500 HR and created an impactful and practical approach to balancing employees' and employers' needs. Central to everything that she does is the belief that all success is accomplished through the dedication and efforts of great employees.

Niki is a firm believer in the powers of collaboration and communication. She carries with her a strong desire to empower employers and their employees to work in partnership to design and implement meaningful workplace and human resources programs rooted in collaboration, respect, trust, and open communication. Niki's ultimate goal is to create a positive ripple in the world, through her unique approach to human resources.

Niki's professional background includes serving in operational management and leadership roles, as a corporate human resources consultant, a community college adjunct faculty, and a human resources executive. In addition to her three HR professional certifications, Niki is bilingual in Spanish/English, holds a Bachelor of Arts degree in Spanish from Arizona State University, and a Master of Business Administration degree in HR management from the University of Phoenix.

About Niki's Company

HRAnswers.org
Human Resources Consulting
https://www.hranswers.org

Be Bold in Your Dreams ...
Stay Strong in Your Pursuit

JW RAYHONS
President

How I Got My Start

Significant impact. Family, freedom, and flexibility. Over the years, I've learned that the reasons you start a business are different from what you experience owning a business. In high school, I knew I wanted to own my own business. Growing up with a dad in construction, we saw firsthand the impact of companies laying you off the moment the project was done and they didn't need you anymore. It caused me to believe that the only way to have freedom, be available for my family, and provide for them was to own a company, not work for a company. I just didn't have any idea what it would be.

My first company was started to help people's most significant dreams become reality. I figured the best way to help people realize that money is not the real thing they want was to start an organization that would help them with the money part of their life. Rayhons Financial was born. What I didn't realize at the time was what an impact it would have in people's lives (including my own). When you put other people's dreams ahead of achieving your own, something paradoxical happens; you end up achieving more in life than you imagined.

The experiences of owning a business are far richer than even the reasons you started the business in the first place. Be bold. Stay strong. Enjoy!

My Advice to Aspiring Business Owners and Entrepreneurs

Starting a business is like a construction project. You've got a picture in your mind of what it will look like, but it will probably end up taking twice as long to build; cost twice as much; have delays, hiccups, and things get in your way; and have many changes to the project itself. It will require blood, sweat, and tears. You'll pour more of yourself into it than you ever imagined. It will test who you are and how bad you want it. And, it will all be worth it.

Your business has the potential to contribute more to your life than you could ever contribute to it. Done right, the team you build and the clients you serve will contribute to who you become. You'll get to experience things that, currently, are beyond your imagination. You'll build relationships with people you never thought you'd get a chance to meet. Being an entrepreneur is tough. You'll have to work for it! It requires fortitude in heavy doses. Be bold in your dreams. Stay strong in your pursuit. Enjoy every moment of your journey. It will all be worth it!

About JW

JW is husband to Tiffany and dad to Michayla, Chase, SJ, and Montana. He is also a business owner, financial advisor, Gallup-Certified Strengths Coach, and board leader. In these roles, JW has had the opportunity to effectively coach clients by helping them discover, acknowledge, and embrace their deepest drivers of success; in other words, their strengths. He is often referred to as authentic, growth-oriented, and values-based. JW's Gallup Top Five CliftonStrengths are achiever, developer, positivity, responsibility, and empathy.

JW is the founder and president of both Rayhons Financial and Joshua Development. It has been his life's work to help others embrace their current place in time and to proactively plan for their future happiness. Experience has confirmed that JW's coaching and career expertise lends itself well to business owners, executives, professionals, community leaders, and other individuals looking for guidance and training in their pursuit of a values and strengths-based approach to their well-being.

Rayhons Financial is consistently ranked in the top seven percent of investment firms within Voya Financial Advisors. JW has been honored with several awards, including Gilbert's 2015 Business Man of the Year, Gilbert's 2016 Volunteer of the Year, Gilbert's 2019 Spirit of Business, and Arizona Business Leaders 2020 Wealth Management. Gilbert, Arizona, is a community with over 250,000 residents. He has served as chair of the board for three organizations and has enjoyed coaching basketball for over four hundred young athletes.

JW's mantra is, "When you look for the good in someone; you'll find it."

About JW's Company
Rayhons Financial, LLC, and Joshua Development, LLC
Disciplined Financial Planning; Investments and Organizational Consulting, Training, and Coaching
www.RayhonsFinancial.com
www.JoshuaDevelopment.com

Get an Education in the Business of Business Ownership

JOAN R. F. ROBINSON

I Am #The Dog-Vocate, LLC

How I Got My Start

I started my business because I wanted to bring a common place to people from all over the world who otherwise might have nothing in common. As a young child growing up in Berkeley, California, I witnessed all types of people from all walks of life gather at Ohlone Dog Park and lose themselves in one another's conversation via the joy of sharing information and the common love of dogs. At this place was where I first witnessed a woman perfectly communicate with her dog with sign language. She was so pleasant and barely uttered a word.

I chose the platform of LinkedIn because, unlike Facebook, it reaches businesspeople all over the world. And it is free of cost. With the idea that people who are working are in unnatural environments, the brain is always seeking to reach a place of homeostasis when it is faced with unpleasant circumstances. I have been employed in one capacity or another since I was fourteen years old and could obtain a work permit. It has been my experience that human beings can be abusive in the work environment. And the mind searches for a place to self-soothe in an attempt to remain calm under extreme stress.

Looking at the image of a dog releases the hormone oxytocin from the brain into the bloodstream, which, in turn, makes the individual experience the swooning feeling of being "in love." With this feeling, it relaxes the individual and brings the brain the homeostasis it was searching for during the onslaught of the human experience.

In my experience with dogs, what I have observed as the number one missing activity from their lives is being taken for a walk on a daily basis. One of the main reasons I see for this lack is that the humans who love dogs are so exhausted from the regular rigors of life that there is no energy left by the time they get home. And the dog walk gets put on the back burner, day after day. A dog must be trained to walk on a leash. If the owners don't consistently practice with their dogs and apply the proper walking techniques, it becomes a tiresome nightmare for all parties involved. Music affects the entire body and can energize people to the degree that they want to go ahead and take that twenty-minute walk. So I upload songs that a playlist can be built from to get the dog owner up and out of the house.

As a black female in the United States, several times a day I am faced with unpleasant situations where I am being talked down to, provoked, lied about or to, or there is someone being suspicious of my goings to and fro, or I'm treated with blatant hatred, such as eye rolling, huffing and puffing, glaring eyes, crossing the street when I approach, phrases like "Why did you say it like that?" "Are you okay?" by people who I have never met before because of the color of my skin. Dogs don't share these feelings. They only know scent and energy. I believe they were created to equalize the energy of human beings. They will love you no matter what you look like.

My Advice to Aspiring Business Owners and Entrepreneurs

The one piece of advice I would give to a person who wants to start a business is to go and take a college-level business class. Learn what a target market is and stick to it. In business class, just like mathematics, you will learn formulas to match your vision. You will learn what to focus on for success and what can throw you off. You will explore what your passion is, and you will find that as you practice what it is that brings you deep inner peace of mind. In class, you will meet other like-minded people who are just as excited about your passion as you are and can give you fuel and new language to support your idea.

In business class, you will learn different aspects of the business you wish to pursue and how best to achieve your goals. You will learn rules and tricks of the trade that if you tried on your own might take years of wasted time. For example, I discovered that it is best to incorporate other professional and well-renowned trainers in my site because people already have a trusted history of experience with these trainers. It is also free ad space for the known trainers on my site and that is always appreciated by them.

In business class, you learn what your strongest traits are and what you might need to hire someone else to do. For example, the creative credit for my website is credited to the world-renowned *Guinness World Records 2016* holder, model Sean O'Pry. It is simple, elegant, and easy to navigate. It also incorporates two of my passions, dogs and fashion.

About Joan

 When Joan was ten years old living in Berkeley, California, her dad brought home a female German Shepherd. He did not have her spayed. Over the next ten years, she had ten litters, consisting of at least five puppies each. And in those years, some of her pups had pups too. Joan was placed in charge of the pups and learned from a young age how to communicate with dogs in an "out of the box" form of thinking. She learned that the single most challenging aspect of working with the behavior of dogs was getting the humans' attention and holding it long enough to teach them how to best love a dog. To show them the motions to move the dog's energy to a place of zero anxiety.

The conversation human beings have with canines is telepathic. Dogs learn how to speak humans' language through their will. The dogs feel the meanings of the spoken words. They smell the hormones that humans emit. And they are guided by all of the human being. Joan helps people to understand what the dog is saying. She trains people the language of the dog. "Fifty shades" of discipline before affection.

The dog language is essentially love language. Intense feeling combined with gestures.

When Joan is with dogs, she barely speaks. People love music . . . and she uses music to pull them to her to hold their attention long enough to teach them how to love. With each song and video, Joan dives into the recesses of the human to help them recall the song and associate the dog behavior information she have attached to it. People start to incorporate her methods, as they work like magic. People feel the love of God's divine work surge through them. They smile.

Joan loves all living things and wishes to share her knowledge of how to get along with the things she understands best..

About Joan's Company
The Dog-Vocate, LLC®
Health and Wellness, Dog Handling, Internet-Based
https://joanofarcrobinson.wixsite.com/thedogvocate

People Care Most About Who You Are, Not What You Sell

SAMANTHA "SAM" ROOT

Owner, Your Real Estate Group, Lujo Commercial Services, and JustWalkInFaith.com

How I Got My Start

Easy ... just kidding. Rather an effortless answer. I created my own company so it would allow my kids to see a tangible legacy; one they could be proud of. One of my biggest fears in life has always been that I would pass away and they would be alone (outside of their dad being around). So I have made it my mission to do enough good in the world serving others in hopes that if I died people I helped would tell my kids how I helped make their life even a slight bit better at my funeral. They would take it upon themselves to make sure my kids were always taken care of however big or small the need.

Helping others is effortless. I was given the blessing of 97 percent empathy for others. From a business capacity, the people business never goes out of style and leaves ripples that will last our loved ones' lifetimes. Kindness is free.

In July 2019, I quit my C-level position and went from six figures to nothing in less than twenty-four hours. Why, you might ask. The owner and I grew apart and had different visions for what each of our legacies would be. I have never been, and will never be, driven by money. I am driven by human beings and helping them learn about themselves so they can make the impossible happen. My job no longer offered this and no longer valued this.

Quitting was not scary, but it was peaceful. I had finally allowed room for God. He had my back and has provided in so many ways since then. "You will be provided for" was the clear-as-day conviction laid on my heart.

I have weaknesses, y'all! Like a ton. I also have severe depression and anxiety. I take mood stabilizers daily. Yep! Sometimes, I need to take a few hours to stay hidden under the covers, but guess what? I get my butt up at ten A.M. to take over the world! You know why I share this? Because many people need to know that yes, you can still run a company, have a life (even kids), and be a mess all mixed into one human body! I have learned it makes entrepreneurship much more fun and I tend to attract all the "cool people." By cool, I mean the perfectly imperfect ones—my client and friends tribe!

August 2019, I got over the sadness of leaving amazing employees behind and I knew I had what it took to flip the industry on its head in a great way. I am now a world changer. Not planet Earth, but my immediate world. The day-to-day people I come in contact with.

I am a thirty-seven-year-old mother of five kids, who are nineteen, eighteen, sixteen, five, and two. They are all biologically mine, in case you're wondering. I am the blessed owner of a real estate company, full-time, and own and operate a standards and process consulting firm.

Leaving my job allowed me to make my own "boss rules." The most important rule for me was living by a slogan I have had for ten years. I just never did anything with it except keep it on a blog I have. "Faith Driven. People Inspired."

If that scares you away up front, then I am glad. It means you would not like me once you meet me. Every single thing I do is with heart in mind. I work daily for someone much greater than myself. When you are faith driven, there is no room for selfish motives. There is certainly no room for bad integrity. I want to make God proud. I am people inspired because it's just who I am. Plain and simple.

My slogan is my compass, and it has brought me joy, peace, financial success, and so much more! The impossible happens more days than not. I know I am on the right path.

My Advice to Aspiring Business Owners and Entrepreneurs
Own your stripes! Do not wear a single feather in your hat that is not authentically you. When it comes to you on a humanistic level, do not compromise those stripes. There is no gray, there cannot be any gray. I promise, there is enough business for any business in today's day and age to be selective in whom you do business with. You must see the big picture. If you want a short-term business, go after any

yahoo—someone who does not share the values and mission of your company. (But if that is the case, do not get into entrepreneurship ... just my two cents, because you'd be wasting your time.)

But, if you are looking to make this your life's legacy work, then interview those prospective clients as much as they interview you. They must be folks you could use a reference twenty-four hours a day, seven days a week. They must be people you could invite (hypothetically or actually) to your home to eat tacos.

People do not care what you sell or what you do. They sincerely care who you are as a human being. This means they will enjoy knowing what your tidy house looks like behind the staircase closet. This means they want to know you struggle with depression and yet run a business. They will love to know that you might or might not be a millionaire. You must know what you define to be success and then strive toward that, letting people watch the journey and process. They want you to ask for what you need, so they can lift you up and support you along the way. (This means through sales, campaign awareness, encouragement, etc.)

There is a reason, ultimately, why you chose to defy gravity and not work for someone else, so it is your job to take people on that journey with you. A few things will happen. They will see you are more than just camera filters. You get to be yourself and not feel the need to pop a new head on and off like a Barbie doll.

Most important, people will find a need within what you offer to buy whatever you are selling (if it is a for-profit business or a for-a-cause business). They will promote you, share your posts, and talk about you in a good way. They will be your ride-or-die tribe.

About Samantha

Samantha "Sam" Root possesses goals and aspirations the size of Texas. The Texas native is owner of Your Real Estate Group and recently launched Lujo Commercial Services, a woman- and minority-owned, full-service commercial standardization and processes company, and has also been a blog writer for ten years.

Sam has been a licensed realtor for fifteen years. She began her real estate career in Texas. For the past twelve years, she, her husband, and three children have been Arizona residents. It was during this time that the Root clan grew from three to five children. Three years ago, after making a family decision to stay permanently in Arizona and not move back to Texas, she earned her Arizona real estate license.

Sam is an active member of West & Southeast Realtors of the (WeSERV) and participates on its committees. She is a member of National Association of Realtors® (NAR) and The Dallas, Texas, Association of Realtors® (METROTEX) along with running The Networking Table Meetup group.

On the commercial real estate side, Sam is a member of AZCREW (she sits on the Professional Development committee), International

Facility Management Association (IFMA), Arizona Business Leadership (AzBL), and a past board member of the Building Owners and Managers Association (BOMA). She was an active committee chair for seven of the ten years she participated.

Away from work, Sam enjoys reading, cooking, and creating strategy and marketing plans for businesses she is passionate about. She enjoys spending quality time with her family and friends and is a coffee lover!

Sam runs free marketing workshops throughout the Arizona Valleys to help inspire others to share their stories through her vulnerable sharing. She believes that if you live authentically vulnerable, your business and personal life will flourish in ways you never thought possible. She is on a mission to create a community of world changers, one person at a time. Sam is fluent in both English and Spanish. In her own words, "I am bilingual 2000 percent."

About Samantha's Company
Your Real Estate Group, Lujo Commercial Consulting, Residential Real Estate Services, Commercial Industry Services Consulting
https://samantharoot.fathomrealty.com

Give No Power to Your Doubts

ELAINE SIMPSON
Consultant • Speaker • Author

How I Got My Start

I began working in the multifamily/property management industry in 1986 and worked my way from being leasing consultant to vice president (VP) of development. My job as the VP of development was to find land, purchase it, and oversee construction efforts through certificate of occupancy. I was great at my job and enjoyed it tremendously, but then the 2007 Great Recession hit, and I was laid-off from my job. I was a single mother and was devastated.

I thought long and hard about what I liked about my previous positions, what kinds of tasks and responsibilities that interested me and made me feel empowered. I realized I loved problem solving, motivating, teaching, and coaching people. I love a good challenge and love the feeling of success, not just for me but also for those I worked with who succeeded. But I also knew that the only industry I knew was property management and construction. How could I combine all this not only into a job but also a career?

The only way to find the career I had created in my mind was not to look outward but to look inward. I cashed in a few investments and founded what is known today as Occupancy Solutions, LLC. I worked at my kitchen table developing my plan and began reaching out to people I knew in the property management industry, letting them know I was open for business. It was a slow start and often I thought I was an imposter but kept moving forward with encouragement from friends and family. Failure was not an option.

I started getting calls from potential clients, which eventually turned into jobs, some small and others even smaller, but it was work. Today, thirteen years later, we are a national company with a team of soluttions specialists providing a variety of services, consulting, education, and so much more to property management and hospitality professionals throughout the United States.

Believe in yourself and your ability because when you doubt your powers, you give power to your doubts.

My Advice to Aspiring Business Owners and Entrepreneurs
Taking the leap from our safe nine-to-five job into the world of entrepreneurship can be terrifying, overwhelming, and challenging, to say the least. Leaving us feeling lonely, lacking confidence, and feeling as if we are swimming upstream . . . alone. As women in a situation such as this, we often do not feel confident and don't believe we can achieve our goals, especially when venturing out to start a

new business of our own and leaving the comforts of our nine-to-five job and that guaranteed paycheck. Even when those around us, family and friends, support us and believe in us, our inner voice is whispering, or in some cases yelling, questions and putting doubts into our heads that sound similar to, "Is this a good idea?" or "What if it is not a good idea?" or "What if it is a good idea and I screw it up and I fail?"

We lack the confidence because we suffer from imposter syndrome, which is a psychological pattern in which we doubt our accomplishments and have a persistent internalized fear of being exposed as a fraud. Despite external evidence of our competence, many of us experiencing this phenomenon remain convinced that we are frauds, and do not deserve all we have achieved or have coming to us. We incorrectly attribute our success as luck or to others who have contributed or supported us along the way, not to our own abilities. We have to stop thinking this way and just do it! When we have this self-doubt, we are sabotaging ourselves and ultimately our success!

If our friends and family believe in us, why shouldn't we believe in ourselves? We should have faith in our abilities, thinking strategically and positively to amaze the world.

About Elaine

Elaine Simpson founded Occupancy Solutions to provide operations, marketing, sales and leasing, training, and consulting services in the multifamily and hospitality industries throughout the United States.

Occupancy Solutions, LLC, has provided services, keynotes, and workshops on property and hospitality management since 1986. Occupancy Solutions assists clients by providing proven, cost-effective techniques and strategies that achieve increased income and reduced vacancies.

Elaine is a passionate national speaker, consultant, trainer, and author with offices in Detroit, Michigan, and Phoenix, Arizona. Her passion for speaking and helping others began early on, and it has stayed with her ever since. As an identical twin within a set of triplets born on Christmas Day, Elaine has always strived to stand out and goes above and beyond to create plans, strategies, workshops, trainings, and keynote presentations that are unique, energizing, and equally as engaging. She shares her positive and not-so-positive stories about being a triplet, possessing thirty-plus years in property management, and being a seasoned road warrior,

Elaine uses her experiences, struggles, successes, and stories—the good, bad, and ugly—to connect and relate to anyone who has customers and/or employees. With humor and interactive exercises, Elaine grabs the audience and takes it for a ride that people will enjoy, remember, and learn from. Elaine is on a mission to inspire individuals, teams, and their leaders to fully realize the positive impact they have on their residents, guests, one another, and the organizations they build.

Elaine is a member of the National Speakers Association; a certified John Maxwell coach, trainer, and speaker; and a National Apartment Association Education Institute facilitator. Additionally, she is a licensed real estate broker in Michigan and Arizona and a certified Seniors Real Estate Specialist®.

About Elaine's Company

Occupancy Solutions, LLC
We provide consulting, training, and services for the property management and hospitality management industries.
www.occupancysolutions.com

Resist Returning to What's Comfortable ... Push Forward

KRISTINA SWIFT

Former Corporate Executive • CEO/Founder of Serendipity Executive Search

How I Got My Start

My parents had their own business—my dad, Wayne Pell, was a chiropractor and my mom, Hope, managed the business. I had a front seat to what it takes and all the sacrifices you make to build a big business. My parents were amazing role models and instilled the importance of work ethic into my sister, Sheree Pell, and me. Most of my career I have trained, supported, and cheered on entrepreneurs and I have always thought someday, it would be my turn.

The time came when I was a sales executive working in a primarily male-led company. I was appalled on a daily basis at the way women were spoken to, treated, and disrespected. I will never forget in the middle of a meeting, one of the male presidents walked in late and ordered me to get out of my chair, because it was his. I thought he was joking until he said, "No, you can move and sit somewhere else." I looked across at the owners, both male, and they just looked down at their notebooks. They allowed him to humiliate me in front of about twenty-five people without saying a word.

During the time I was there, I built strong relationships, hired top talent, launched new programs and initiatives, saved the company money, and implemented new processes—in essence I did my job well. One day, my newly hired younger male boss let me go without cause, and I was walked out the door. My also female boss (his boss), who was one of the only other female executives, was let go without cause on the phone at the same time. For both of us, this was shocking.

She and I had excellent reputations in our industry and had never had anything like this happen. Her daughter and my son were both working at the company that day and we had to call them before someone else told them their moms were let go. It was traumatic. That day we both agreed, "No more bosses." I let this horrible experience fuel my passion to continue to help people and add value to companies on my own terms. My disclaimer in this story is that I worked for incredible companies filled with people who took the time to develop my skills and coach me along my career journey. They are still an inspiration to me today, and they were the first to trust me with their talent searches. I am so grateful for them. A big thank you goes to Angie Rossi, Eddie Silcock, Travis Garza, and Janice Jackson for not only being amazing ambassadors in our industry but also for being servant Leaders who invested in me and who believed in me.

The world needs more people like you, and I plan to pay it forward to up and coming entrepreneurs who seek guidance, wisdom, and support.

I decided that I never wanted to be in a position to let someone else determine my worth, my value, and, most important, my ability to be successful. I started my own executive recruiting business—helping people find their dream jobs and companies find top talent for their executive teams. I no longer have the pit in my stomach on the way to work, I have lost the continuous conflicted feeling of misalignment with my values and integrity. I am free! I am successful! I am becoming a badass!

I had been successful for twenty-four years in the same industry and I share my story because you will have your own set of deal breakers that challenge you to question whether what you are doing is really enabling you to reach your full potential. You will have that defining moment just like I did, and you will make a change. You will be tempted to get pulled back into what you know, what you are comfortable doing and good at. Resist and push forward because take it from me; you haven't even scratched the surface of what you are capable of when you are in charge of your destiny. In six months, I have replaced that corporate income, and I know I will exceed it. I meet incredible people every day and have met companies and executives that I truly admire and am honored to do work for.

My Advice to Aspiring Business Owners and Entrepreneurs

Starting your own business is not easy and requires a certain level of perseverance and grit. One of the realizations that came to me fast is that I am no longer the decision-maker, so I have had to strengthen my patience level. I am at the mercy of the pace of the companies I partner with. In essence, when you are dealing with people, you have to meet them where they are, and pushing past that will put your outcome in jeopardy.

Practice patience and believe that things will happen exactly the way they are meant to. You have to be willing to hustle, network, and prospect to be successful—work it like your life depends on it. When you are building, it is not easy—it requires you to do whatever it takes. Embrace the disappointments, learn from them because they are part of the journey. They build character and make you appreciate the wins. Ask for advice from other like-minded entrepreneurs who have gone before you—learn from them. Follow on social entrepreneurs you admire—I am obsessed with Sara Blakely, the founder of Spanx; she is a constant reminder of what is possible. Fill your feeds with positivity and empty the tank of negativity. Surround yourself with people who support you and be willing to walk away from people who don't. Set goals. Don't give up. Get back up. Practice resilience and discipline.

Be careful not to get lost in "mindset" and personal development that you are not taking enough action—you get paid on the daily action you take that moves you closer to your goals—that takes precedence over anything else. A lot of personal development will come "on the job" as you perfect your craft. Keep moving—keep connecting!

About Kristina

Kristina Swift was born and raised in Ontario, Canada. Her entrepreneurial spirit started young. Her family lived beside a golf course. She picked up all the golf balls that landed on their property and sold them back to the driving range. This was her first small business.

Kristina moved to the US. At the age of twenty-six, she started working for Avon Products as an entry-level sales manager and worked her way up to become head of sales of her home country, Canada. After an eighteen-year career with Avon, she joined Stella & Dot, LLC, and had the chance to work for the CEO and founder Jessica Herrin, an industry icon entrepreneur. Kristina was the vice president of sales at Isagenix and the senior vice president of sales at Plexus Worldwide in Arizona, where she lives today. She launched Serendipity Executive Search in the fall of 2019.

Her son, Ethan Meeks, graduated from Grand Canyon University with a business degree and is working in the same industry his mom spent her career in. Kristina and her partner live in Scottsdale, Arizona. She attributes much of her freedom and success to Matt Justice—his unwavering belief and support in her and the time and grace to build Serendipity. It was meant to be.

About Kristina's Company

Serendipity Executive Search

Executive Placement

www.serendipityexecutivesearch.com

Focus on What You Uniquely Do and Delegate the Rest

AMBER TAGGARD
Professional Organizer

How I Got My Start

After nearly a decade of struggling with infertility, my husband and I were finally able to have a baby: a sweet little bald guy we named Ryan. During the years that went by before he came along, I made good use of my time by completing a Master of Science degree in clinical mental health and embarking on a career in higher education, which I truly loved. I loved it so much, that when Ryan was born, we got a trusted in-home sitter and I went back to work . . . for about three months.

The mental image I'd cooked up—business suits and presentations by day, pumping in my office to keep my breastmilk supply up, seamlessly transitioning to mommy mode the minute work was done and being perfectly fine to drop baby off with the sitter again the next morning—didn't pan out. The reality looked a lot more like a spit-up stain on my suit jacket, painfully learning that my breasts didn't want to experience letdown for a machine like they did a baby, realizing that I was worried about the baby when I was at work and worried about work when I was with baby, and I was in tears each morning as I dropped my little guy off.

And then one day, it happened ... a text from my sitter with a video of Ryan rolling over unassisted for the first time. Logically, I had known ahead of time that this would likely happen. Other people would experience his firsts and that would be okay, I'd told myself. It would be okay and he would be okay and I would be okay. And I was. Right up until I wasn't. The reality that I had missed this milestone and that I would keep missing them, one after the next after the next, slapped me like ocean waves lapping at the shore. And that was when I knew that I was going to demand more. That I was going to refuse to accept the idea that we all have to just tuck our lives in around the edges of our careers and hope for the best. That I was going to let someone or something else dictate how I spent the precious nonrenewable resource that is time.

My Advice to Aspiring Business Owners and Entrepreneurs

When I first started my business, I, like most small business owners, did every last thing. I answered the phone. I went to the post office. I sent invoices. I did the bookkeeping, you name it. And I did this for years! A true changing point in the trajectory of my business came when I took a step back and asked myself what, of all the things that I ran around doing each day, could uniquely be done by me. Could I email an invoice in a super special way that no one else could duplicate? Was my professional experience required to run errands? Did my extensive education enable me to keep up with my profit and loss like no one else could? No. Nah. Nope.

"What can uniquely be done by me?" Honestly answering this question and setting aside any desire to not be too prideful to unlock a wealth of information. For me, I knew that no one else could network about my company like I could. I have more understanding and experience in my own business than anyone on the planet. I'm passionate about it and I believe in it.

I also knew that no one could train new organizers like I could. I knew what personality traits and skill sets I was looking for, and I uniquely knew what processes and methods I wanted my crew members to be taught. I also knew that no one else could handle public speaking engagements like I could. I naturally enjoy speaking and can bring energy and legitimacy to the subject by speaking from my experience and education.

Focusing on what I could uniquely do allowed me to choose to delegate all other tasks. It was a big leap and it was scary because it meant relinquishing two key things: control and money, but it set me free to focus on the areas where my particular experience, education, and personality could offer the best return on investment (ROI), and that has made all the difference.

About Amber

Amber Taggard, owner and founder of The Organizer Chicks, is a professional organizer, time-management coach, and public speaker. She holds a Master of Science in Clinical Mental Health, and she is passionate about using her counseling psychology background to help people improve their mental health and productivity through creating organized spaces. Amber believes that our physical spaces affect every part of our lives, and she wants to help others utilize the power of organization to live thriving lives. Amber and her husband Justen have four children, and they love living in Northwest Arkansas.

About Amber's Company

The Organizer Chicks
Professional Organizers
www.theorganizerchicks.com

Stay Lit Up About What You Do

HOPE PHILLIPS UMANSKY, PhD
Specialty Educational Consultant • Speaker on Revolutionary
Education Reform

How I Got My Start

"You've always had the power . . . [You] had to learn it for
[yourself]."
— Glinda the Good Witch, *The Wizard of Oz* movie, 1939

My mom always said, "The only thing you can never lose in your life
is your education. Money comes and goes; relationships change;
children grow and leave. You can lose your house, job, and relationship, but no one can ever take your education away from you." She
was a career educator and much of what I know about being a
servant leader in education is from having watched her while growing
up, coloring in the back of board and faculty meetings, listening to

her teach English literature to students, tutoring them in writing, and enacting the characters from the books to bring them to life for her students. All the fun she had with them and connection. My heart knew, I was an educator. Education is something that grows deep inside and integrates with who you are. All else is transitory. What remains is our character, how we have educated ourselves about the world, and the people inside it. Thus, I wanted to teach, write, and live a relatively quiet, no-pressure life. That's why I always referred to myself as the "accidental CEO" of a private graduate school.

First and always, I am a writer, a teacher, a lover of words, and a helper of students finding their voices and the confidence to succeed. People have said I am a bit "touched," special in the way that I can watch a commercial and weep, or watch the news and cry, and then feel joy and laugh at the next show. I feel the human condition deeply. Writing this in 2020, my heart is shattered for humanity while also rooting for our resilience, our love of one another, and, of course, for hope. Wishing in the deepest deep of my heart that this will be the precipice of change, using our despair and outrage to mark this moment of our heart's reopening to others.

This heart-centered space of hopefulness and potential is why I fell in love with the field of education, even after training to be a psychologist. I returned to the warm halls of academia, the beautiful engaging family communities that were schools. Nothing is as transformative as a solid education, and that has nothing to do with the degree itself. The real education comes from the lessons between the lines, the things we learn while living or doing the schoolwork: the empathy, the altruism, the philanthropy of spirit, and the great resilience of human beings.

Only an education can transform not just an individual's life but the lives of the family he or she has yet to have and all the generations of elders that came before. That's an incredible legacy to have by helping guide students toward meaningful educational pathways. If there were ever a time to reinvent myself professionally, move into the public sector of my industry to catalyze the movement that I envision, it is now. Apparently, I was a trendsetter, separating myself out from all I no longer needed and hopefully paralleling the country's own moment to reset and reimagine itself.

When I formerly joined the administrative ranks from teaching to become, first, a dean to getting the rare lifetime achievement of being appointed as a chief executive officer (CEO), I quickly learned that all the creativity and passion that got me there was not welcome to live among the compliance, accreditation, curriculum, problem solving, ever negotiating, board managing, firefighting (yes, one time), policy clarifying, revising, and writing that goes on all day, every day. Even an email is a complex negotiation, a potential power play about who is or is not included, blindly, copied, and vividly.

Every year, my professional identity, the professor, who was inspired to write funny, witty, deep lectures comparing current events, historical context, pop culture, film, and literature together to teach and move students was fading. The creative soul in me, the humanitarian spirit, was feeling compromised with the shifting priorities of higher education. Do not let its veneer fool you. Higher education is cutthroat. Get donors or die! Fundraise or perish! Find those tuition drivers or fade away! The CEO role began with leading a campus through aspirational goals and close interpersonal coaching of students' whole selves, interfacing with faculty, boards, the public, and academic experts who, over time, became comrades and friends toward pursuing a mission. Then, seemingly overnight, it became all about fundraising and compliance, which left me feeling stifled and trapped, like the bird in a gilded cage.

"She's only a bird in a gilded cage,
A beautiful sight to see,
You may think she's happy and free from care,
She's not, though she seems to be."
—Words by Arthur J. Lamb, music by Harry Von Tilzer
"A Bird in the Gilded Cage," 1900

Apparently, an unwritten rule circulated on a memo that did not make it to my inbox: as a woman, you seemingly have an obligation to over-perform if you make it to the C-suite. If you manage to slip through the crack of the glass ceiling you popped out of, now you have to stay. Representing in the C-suite for women, you have to show well. If you cry, feel, emote, that is no good. You don't want to be perceived as weak or the dreaded, "too emotional," "too invested." Too parental, even with your own. If firing a person turns your blood cold and makes you vomit, churning at your insides for weeks leading up to the moment because you know the implications your words will have are life-changing, do not mention your reticence or care. Just do it. Suck it up. People say it is lonely at the top. If you cannot do it, someone else will without an issue.

To be sure, whether man or woman in the C-suite, you will lose the popularity contest; whatever move you make is second-guessed. You must be always loyal and proper. First, of course to the institution and uphold a private and reserved persona aligned with the institutional mission. The shine started to wear away. The way a relationship does when the bloom comes off the rose; when you think, *Am I being gaslit? What is happening that I am not seeing?* The idea that I was playing it small snuck up on me at quiet moments.

When I experienced the power of being able to pull a community together by speaking publicly and extemporaneously for a mission, a purpose that comes from the heart, the thought came that maybe I could be doing more. If this comes so easy, speaking boldly, publicly, and from the heart about education, if I can compel people with my rogue vision and authenticity here in this sphere, couldn't I do more to help underserved, underrepresented, and undereducated groups? My vision helped students with whom I worked and elevated the brand to mean something to people, but couldn't my views as an institutional leader, values such as human kindness, academic integrity, and student-centrism—now seen as rogue, front-lined initiatives in this climate—make a difference in the higher education landscape? Instead of talking about students as tuition drivers and enrollment markers, my vision was simple: a return to humanity in education.

Make no mistake, what is playing out on the world stage is connected to the past few decades of systematic divestment of the arts, literature (uncensored and unredacted), and non-revisionist history in education. Inevitably, it is blamed on a perceived "lack of funding" and feigns under a façade of political correctness that parades as inclusive, but insidiously perpetuates exclusion, discrimination, and inequality. As a field, we are so far from where we originated as a cultivator of the human spirit, creativity, beauty, and invention, it can be disheartening, but what if I could form a movement, have a platform, to speak about this issue? It nagged at me to not play small anymore.

This past spring, a few months before my departure, I was walking the halls in the early evenings, making sure the campus was ready before the students descended and a sing-song memory of childhood came back to me. It was of my mom softly singing to me before bed, when I was upset, about my name. According to her, it was the most important name in the world. She showed me that hope is the greatest thing in all of history, literature, and the arts. Never being one to tone down expectations, she would say, "It is a big name to live up to; don't forget you don't play it small." Now, in the recesses of my mind, I see her down on her knees putting a bandage on mine, and I can hear her sing-song her favorite poem.

"'Hope' is the thing with feathers—
That perches in the soul—
And sings the tune without the words—
And never stops—at all—"
　　　　—Emily Dickinson, "'Hope' Is the Thing with Feathers," 1861

The culmination of my life's tragic and triumphant experiences and education had brought me to this moment. Something stirred; I would be open to the charge, to the call, when/if I got it. The cognitive dissonance became real. As spring turned to summer, my heart started to shatter, and I remembered that the Tin Man had been sternly warned by the Wizard of Oz that a heart was not an easy thing to have.

"As for you, my galvanized friend, you want a heart. You don't know how lucky you are not to have one. Hearts will never be practical until they can be made unbreakable."

—The Wizard of Oz, *The Wizard of Oz* movie, 1939

That is when I thought, "Okay, Dr. Hope, regroup. You have done this before. No one says you have to stay." When women hear that you left, you resigned from a CEO position, especially in higher education, they ask, "Oh my gosh, you left? Why would you do that? What happened?" It is almost as if it is a micro-betrayal, a small cut in your allegiance to sisterhood. You somehow squeaked by, you somehow got in, and then you left? You broke the glass ceiling and now have left it in a pile of dust. Only a few get through. How could you?

There are some things worth not compromising your vision. One is your heart. Advocacy for student rights and the student experience is most important to me. Wherever we are in life, if our creativity won't spark, if we find ourselves crawling back into ourselves, it is time to regroup. No title is worth your essence.

"The caged bird sings
with a fearful trill
of things unknown
but longed for still
and his tune is heard
on the distant hill
for the caged bird
sings of freedom,"

—Maya Angelou, "The Caged Bird," 1983

Angelou affirmed that the great metaphor is resilience and a boundless spirit. In 2020, more important, the question is not so much why the caged bird sings, but does she have to? I mean, especially, while she's in the cage?

One day, I did what I did not think I could do and left the CEO role. One day, the sparkle dust entered just right, flickering between the gaps in the bars, to show me where the light was to enter the unknown, that there was air to breathe out there, and one day that was like any other day was not, and I just let it all go.

"Ultimately, man should not ask what the meaning of his life is, but rather he must recognize that it is *he* who is asked. In a word, each man is questioned by life; and he can only answer to life by *answering for* his own life; to life he can only respond by being responsible."
—Viktor E. Frankl, *Man's Search for Meaning,* 1946

There was no crawling back through the small hole left in the ceiling that I was now standing on, no chance of backing out like a kid, butt first stuck in a one-way tunnel, trying to get my body through the small, jagged hole back to the other side. When that did not work, I imagined reversing that still, like a kid trying to dive back to the simplicity of uncut glass, and I could not get back through. It was impossible, every time making the bleep, soft sound of an object bouncing back into the vortex as some actions can never be undone. It is a one-way ceiling, for sure.

Picturing myself invincible as a little girl in my favorite Dorothy of *The Wizard of Oz* costume that I had gotten for my sixth birthday that year and refused to take off, I wondered how you could get so far from home that you have to click your shoes to get back there. I even had the hard, red, patent-leather Mary Janes (and they even had bandage on the soles so I wouldn't slip on the glass slippery surface). I jump up and slam down as hard as I can to crack it. Top to bottom this time; knees up and feet landing together hard. It is this girl's endless potential and belief in herself, as yet unadulterated by life's disappointments, triumphs, and tragedies, so innocent still to think that what finally cracked the glass was to just shatter the whole thing open to take me home again.

In this spirit of reinvigorating the education landscape with a movement to return to a time when both teachers and students are held in high regard and humanity, an awareness of our humanness, I founded Innovations: Education Advocacy Group, Inc., in June 2019. Innovations covers all aspects of global proprietary external and internal initiatives, many of which I have created during my thirteen years in higher education administration and continued teaching, including nontraditional and traditional initiatives, fundraising, alumni drives, and accreditation campaigns. For example, such as leading a Western Association of Schools and Colleges (WASC) effort over a six-year period. Each project, whether short or long term, is as unique as each organization's own culture. Finding the pathways to each school's or organization's sustained legacy is my charge, even through one of the most challenging times in higher education. Often that is accomplished through creation of mission- and student-centered initiatives to reengage stakeholders at all levels through all levels of the institution.

My Advice to Aspiring Business Owners and Entrepreneurs

While the vision, the brand, is forming, do not forget to be authentically you. Do not play small or forget who you are. Haters gonna hate. Elevate, ignore; do not respond. Sir Winston Churchill's 1966 words about education stay front in my mind, "The first duty of a university is to teach wisdom, not trade; character, not technicalities." This is an opportunity that soon will dawn on you. Wait, I am in charge here. You set the terms for every working relationship and contract you have. Now, you are the NASCAR pacesetter, a leader. Be unafraid to step into the leader's shoes with character, empathy, and transparency. No brand, no vision, can sell without a feeling heart behind it who believes in every part of it. Whatever it is that enlivens you, your business and clients deserve no less. Stay lit up about what you do.

In my first few projects, a familiar pattern would emerge where I would forget this. I would switch back to thinking I report to a board, an instituitional body. A switch gets turned after a few times of offering advice to a prospect that should have been under contract or working for less than you deserve (women, hello!) and overperforming for fear of being fired. Then you realize, "What, I am the pacer. I am driving this deal."

"Watch your character, for it becomes destiny," said Frank Outlaw, president of Bi-Lo Stores. And, it's in that moment, you own your agency, that the shift to owner happens.

About Hope

"No schooling was allowed to interfere with my education."

—Grant Allen, 1894

Hope Phillips Umansky spent the last twenty-six years holding different positions in independent and private institutions as faculty, administrator, academic dean, program director, WASC accreditation liaison officer (ALO), and CEO. In June 2019, she was compelled to launch Innovations: Education Advocacy Group, Inc, a consulting practice in higher education management and leadership. Innovations: EAG is distinct in that it creates fully individualized educational management initiatives and strategic plans, without the use of templates or "tried and true" initiatives. Innovations: EAG is singularly student centered and mission aligned; that is the most robust and vigorous growth driver.

Hope has attended and worked at traditional and nontraditional schools and believes that education comes in many ways and forms. She holds a Bachelor of Arts degree in English literature from Scripps College, a Master of Arts degree in liberal studies, English literature, from Reed College, and master's and doctoral degrees in clinical psychology from California Institute for Human Science (CIHS), a boutique graduate institute. Her work at CIHS began in 2010 as associate dean and each year she was appointed with progressively increasing responsibilities as academic dean, WASC ALO, and CEO.

For almost ten years, she led the institution through the WASC process and had unprecedented growth.

Innovations: EAG has a proprietary system for a total overhaul and culture realignment to re-engage students for organic and sustainable growth that is also fully mission aligned. Hope's passions within this work are engaging with students to incite their natural love of learning; conducting professional and faculty development, including creating strategic communication and holding gender, culture, and inclusivity trainings; spending time on campuses experiencing school culture at all levels; managing board communication and development; and engaging internal and external stakeholders in forward-thinking ways. Innovations: EAG's fully customized plans are designed within the school's or organization's culture to create truly forefront internal and external initiatives. A singular focus on the student experience and mission alignment through all levels of the institution advances rigor and success while still honoring the whole student in the contemporary educational landscape.

About Hope's Company
Innovations: Education Advocacy Group, Inc.
Education and Human Potential
www.innovationsadvocacy.com

Get Clear About Values, Motives, Energy, and Passion

KYIRA WACKETT, MS, LPC

Therapist • Speaker • Coach • Artist • Owner Founder of Adversity Rising, LLC, and Kinda Kreative, LLC

How I Got My Start

Like many entrepreneurs, one of the primary drivers for beginning my business was that I did not want to work for someone else. But it was less about needing things to be "my way" or wanting to be in control and more about how I could best address the real shame narrative and layers of anxiety I had been existing in throughout my life. See, I spent years trying to do and be "more" to earn that sense of worthiness and connection with others. I would overextend myself in all I did to try to feel as though I earned the right to call myself "good enough," while feeling burnt out, resentful, and anxious all the time.

I was always trying to be "on top" and struggled getting feedback, dreaded making a mistake, and often found myself investing more energy, time, and interest in the work I was doing than my supervisors, superiors, and, in some cases, even business owners. Over time, this drained my resources and led me to have to make a more difficult decision—to break out of this cycle of shame and anxiety and shift my focus on self-efficacy, self-esteem, and creating products and services that aligned with what I wanted to do and my overall values rather than working to align myself with someone else's "why" and my shame story.

Now, don't get me wrong, these narratives and habits also carried with me into my entrepreneurial pursuits but the role I took and the challenges I faced were internal wounds and stories. In doing this work, it allowed me to better make that shift in my focus and work on rewriting a narrative that I wanted to exist in. Self-doubt, shame, and fear were (and are) still present but I have learned to ground myself more in my "why" and the values I hold, anchoring my work to these roots and allowing myself to be seen for who I am and what I stand for rather than continuing in a path of performance and conformity.

This played into the second motivator for launching my own business—needing a greater variety in my daily schedule and in the work I do. My interests and skills are vast and while I could find jobs that would allow me to pursue some of these pieces, nothing allowed me to create the day-to-day life I was longing for or to tap into each of the areas of my life I wanted to incorporate into my profession in a meaningful way. Multi-passionate is what many people refer to it as— and as an artist, public speaker, facilitator, therapist, and coach, my various passions and skills were too diverse to fit into a predefined category or role.

In working for myself, I can ebb and flow in all these areas and find the mixtures that work best for me. For example, I can take a few weeks and focus solely on painting to gear up for a big art show or take on a role training staff in a mental health facility about how to best address and deal with shame in their clinical work. I can take off on a Tuesday when my husband, who works in emergency medicine, has off or work around my daughter's schedule to be available for whatever she needs.

This is not a life that exists independently of challenges. With it comes a whole new set of shame stories I have had to tackle, but this is the life that best aligns with who I am and gives me the opportunity and flexibility to truly thrive in my personal and professional life.

My Advice to Aspiring Business Owners and Entrepreneurs

I think there are two key pieces everyone needs to address before starting their own business. Find the balance between insight and action and face any insecurities and pain points you have with money. The first is a problem many people face personally and professionally—either rushing to action before they have built up enough insight or understanding of their why or spending too much time in the insight phase, letting their fears and shame guide them into a state of stagnation.

How do you know when you have generated enough insight to move forward? When you have gotten clear about the values, motives, energy, and passion driving you to take on this role and do this work. Anyone can do what they know or are good at, but when you are thinking about starting your own business, you want to find the thing that excites you and will keep you going every day. This is your anchor point and will help distinguish you and the work you do from everyone else in the world. This "why" will also help keep you from experiencing scope creep or the expansion of what you do and offer, diluting your brand and deliverables.

How do I know if I have rushed to action too quickly? Usually, this is a result of a scarcity mindset and/or an external anchoring (focusing your idea of success or progress on the judgment and assessment of those around you). You are starting a business. You are building a brand. Not everything has to be done in one day. You are not supposed to have it all figured out when you start. You are never going to please everyone. You want to focus on creating something that will last and that you can see yourself doing every day, not just the next flashy product or service.

Ask yourself, whenever you are moving to action, who and what you are doing this for. Is it for the approval of others or the need to assert a greater sense of legitimacy? Is it because you are worried about how you will get enough money to make ends meet without the pushing of sales? Is it because your shame narrative, fear, and anxiety have taken over the driver seat? Or is it truly because it aligns with your business model and plan and roots back to your why? And one of the best ways I can think about navigating through this is to create a business plan, complete with a value set, and make sure that everything you say "yes" to or take action on can fit in and align with this document.

Finally, get clear about your relationship with and address any concerns surrounding money. This has to do with feelings of scarcity, how you feel about money, and the ways in which you see your value (in what you do and the product or service you provide) translating to financial worth. The scarcity mindset is real and can lead us to make many decisions in our businesses that do not align with our "why"— spending time, money, and energy on projects and outcomes that we do not believe in or want to be doing, saying "yes" to opportunities we want to say "no" to, working tirelessly and losing ourselves in our shame stories. Get clear about the relationship that you have and stories you have been handed about money. And then work to create one that aligns with how you want to see your business and brand develop. And in terms of your value and worth, it is important to address negative self-talk and worries about judgment you have. Think about how you can separate from these and move to seeing your right to charge what you are worth and separate the reactions and responses from others in doing so.

About Kyira

Kyira Wackett is an artist, public speaker, and community advocate. She holds a master's degree in counseling psychology and is a licensed therapist specializing in eating disorders, anxiety disorders, and trauma.

Kyira has been speaking on topics related to mental health, authenticity, and personal and professional development for over ten years with a focus on assertive communication, shame, and fear and moving from a life of "busy" to "fulfilled." She brings a unique blend of didactic and hands-on learning to all sessions and believes in empowering people to take the "next right step" for themselves and to write the story they want to exist within.

In 2017, her company received an America's Small Business Award, about which Kyira notes she is still in shock but has used to remind herself every day about how important the work is that she is doing.

About Kyira's Company
Adversity Rising, LLC
Public Speaking, Therapy, Facilitation
www.adversityrising.com

About the Compiler

BRIDGETT McGOWEN
International Professional Speaker • Author • Publisher

"Talks too much" was a comment Bridgett McGowen consistently received on her elementary school report cards. Early on, she developed a love for speaking, words, and books—so much so until she was always the first to volunteer to read passages aloud in class, and during moments of boredom in her third- and fourth-grade classes, she would analyze the dictionary, jotting down those words and definitions she found particularly interesting.

With reading as a favorite pastime and little to no fear of speaking in front of a crowd, it only makes sense that Bridgett is now an award-winning international professional speaker and the CEO of BMcTALKS Press, an independent publishing company where she thrives in an environment that positions her to bring other people's words to life. Bridgett's résumé also includes being a 2019-2020 member of Forbes Coaches Council and launching BMcTALKS Academy where, as the founder and owner, she offers online self-paced courses to move professionals to use their voices to monetize their expertise.

But business ownership was not always in her sights. It was in 2016 when she was laid-off from her position with an edtech company that she decided to launch her speaking business, a launch that was due in great part to the encouragement and support of her friend, Kiala Givehand. Bridgett had been on stages for years, though—well before launching BMcTALKS in 2016, well before making presentations for that edtech company, and well before her years of teaching at her alma mater from 2002 until January of 2009.

Since 2001, Bridgett has been a professional speaker, and she has appeared on programs alongside several prominent figures such as former President Barack Obama, Deepak Chopra, Alex Rodriguez (A-Rod), Oprah Winfrey, Shonda Rhimes, Katie Couric, Chip Gaines, and Janelle Monáe.

The prestigious University of Texas at Austin presented her with a Master Presenter Award in 2006; Canada-based One Woman has presented her with two Fearless Woman Awards; and she has facilitated hundreds of workshops, keynote and commencement addresses, conference sessions, trainings, and webinars to thousands of students and professionals who are positioned all around the globe.

Bridgett's expertise and presentations have been sought after by companies, post-secondary institutions, and organizations such as Society for Human Resource Management (SHRM), Vanguard Investments, Norton LifeLock, Symantec, Kentucky Fried Chicken, McGraw-Hill Education, LinkedIn Local, Association for Talent Development (ATD), Doña Ana Community College, North Carolina Chamber of Commerce, National Association of Women Sales Professionals, Independence University, Arizona Private School Association, Turnitin, Texas Healthcare Trustees, National Association of Black Accountants, Greater Phoenix Convention & Visitors Bureau, and Prairie View A&M University.

Forbes, LinkedIn, and Thrive Global are a few of the platforms where you can find articles penned by Bridgett. In addition, she has been quoted by Transizion, has contributed to UpJourney, and has appeared as a guest on The Training and Learning Development Company's TLDCast, Phoenix Business Radio, and a multitude of podcasts to showcase her expertise in the professional speaking industry. Her work has been highlighted by *VoyagePhoenix Magazine*, award-winning Scottsdale-based branding and consulting agency, Catalyst; The Startup Growth; and her alma mater, Prairie View A&M University (PVAMU), the second oldest institution of higher education in the state of Texas and a part of the Texas A&M University System.

Bridgett has also taught for PVAMU, Lone Star College System, and University of Phoenix. She graduated cum laude with her bachelor's degree in communication, and one year later, she graduated summa cum laude with her master's degree. She is a Forbes contributor; a publisher; a member of International Society of Female Professionals; a former member of National Speakers Association; and a member of Alpha Kappa Alpha Sorority, Incorporated.

In 2019, Bridgett authored and published two books, *REAL TALK: What Other Experts Won't Tell You About How to Make Presentations That Sizzle* as well as *Rise and Sizzle: Daily Communication and Presentation Strategies for Sales, Business, and Higher Ed Pros,* the former of which sold out within minutes of her presentation concluding at ATD's 76th annual international conference and exposition in Washington, D.C. and which was also a finalist for a 2020 Next Generation Indie Book Award.

In January 2020, she also wrote and published *Show Up and Show Out: 52 Communication Habits to Make You Unforgettable,* which sold out at the annual Think Better Live Better event hosted in February 2020 in San Diego, California by *New York Times* bestsellers Marc and Angel Chernoff. Days later, she published her first compilation, *Own the Microphone: How 50 of the World's Best Professional Speakers Launched Their Careers (and How You Can, Too!)* Four months later, her second and third compilations, *Triumph Over the Trials* and *Redesign Your 9-to-5*, were published, and her next book project, *A Collective Breath,* and her first podcast are both due for summer 2020 releases.

Bridgett's mission is to work beyond the hours of 9am to 5pm to help scores of professionals turn their words and voices into powerhouses, inspire millions, and build serious skill sets and mindsets that will lead to more and more opportunities.

Bridgett is married to Aaron Hawkins, and he makes her laugh every day. Their family resides in the Phoenix, Arizona area. Bridgett enjoys frequent summertime get-aways to San Diego, and she absolutely loves beautiful sunsets.

About BMcTALKS Press

BMcTALKS Press is an independent publishing company that provides a full suite of publishing services to new authors.

We design, create, and deliver high-quality trade books and eBooks that expand your brand, support your vision, and solidify you as a contender in your industry.

BMcTALKS Press knows professional speakers, professional coaches, entrepreneurs, and small business owners are passionate about what they do. We empower them to realize the expertise, savviness, acumen, and passion they bring to the world, and we assist them with identifying avenues for achieving the goal of becoming published authors.

When you get published, you position yourself to ...
- Add "published author" to your already impressive list of accomplishments
- Establish yourself as an authority and an expert on a topic
- Have a book that serves as an "elevated business card"
- Provide added value to your clients
- Support and expand your brand
- Give your followers another way to connect with you
- Share an important message with the world
- Leave a legacy
- Grow your business
- Make an impact
- Get your message out to the world

Visit **www.bmctalkspress.com** to schedule your complimentary, no-obligation call to discuss your book idea.

Do you already have a completed manuscript?
Submit it to **info@bmtpress.com,** and let us get to work for you. Let's print your passion!